THE COMPLETE WRITER
WRITING WITH EASE
Strong Fundamentals

by
Susan Wise Bauer

Peace Hill Press
www.peacehillpress.com

This book is to be used in conjunction with *The Complete Writer* workbooks

Level 1   ISBN 978-1-933339-26-9
Level 2   ISBN 978-1-933339-29-0
Level 3   ISBN 978-1-933339-30-6
Level 4   ISBN 978-1-933339-31-3

Available at www.peacehillpress.com or wherever books are sold

© 2008 Peace Hill Press

Publisher's Cataloging-In-Publication Data
(Prepared by The Donohue Group, Inc.)

Bauer, Susan Wise.
   Writing with ease : strong fundamentals / by Susan Wise Bauer.

     p. ; cm. -- (Complete writer)

   "This book is to be used in conjunction with The Complete Writer workbooks."
-- t.p. verso.
   Includes bibliographical references and index.
   ISBN: 978-1-933339-25-2

1. English language--Rhetoric--Study and teaching. 2. English language--
Composition and exercises--Study and teaching. I. Title.

LB1576 .B38 2008
372.62/3 2007936541

Contents

————————————— **APPENDICES** —————————————

PART I

UNDERSTANDING THE PROCESS

Why Writing Programs Fail

When I first began teaching literature and writing at the College of William and Mary in Virginia, over ten years ago, my freshmen weren't exactly polished writers. Out of every class of thirty freshmen students, four or five would turn in grammatically correct, coherent, clean papers. Of those, perhaps two would show a real grasp of persuasive writing.

Ten years later, even that percentage has dropped. I read through scores of incoherent, fragmented, unpunctuated papers, written by students who graduated from well-funded high schools with small classrooms and qualified teachers.

What are those students being taught before they get to me?

It's not that they don't write. In fact, in an effort to solve the problem of poor writing skills, schools are giving longer and more complex assignments to younger and younger children. The theory is that the more writing children do, the better they'll get at it; as one proponent of it recently told me, "Give the children high-interest assignments and have them write, write, write and revise, revise, revise." First and second graders are told to write journal entries; third and fourth graders are assigned book reports and essays. Fifth and sixth graders are given research papers.

Meanwhile, writing skills continue to decline. And for the last ten years, at education conferences all across the country, I have heard the same refrain from the parents of these children: *My child hates to write.*

There's a central problem with the write-more-and-you'll-get-better method. It treats writing as though it were analogous to speech: the more deeply you're immersed in it, the more competent you'll become.

But writing is essentially unlike speaking. Children have an instinctual, inborn desire to speak. Any child who is developing normally will learn to speak if spoken to. The more a child talks, the better her verbal skills become.

Children don't have that same innate drive to write. Some children scribble as soon as they can hold a pencil, but the majority don't. Even children who are taught to read and are surrounded by written language do not necessarily learn how to write—because speech and writing are fundamentally different.

Writing, unlike speech, isn't a natural activity. Mankind survived for a very long time without finding it necessary to put anything down on paper. Until the nineteenth century (which is quite late, in the larger scheme of things) even the largest empires chugged along perfectly well with shockingly low literacy rates. Administrators and bureaucrats had to be able to read and write, but the masses functioned quite well without paper and pencil. If they'd been unable to talk, on the other hand, their country would have fallen apart.

Written language is an unnatural foreign language, an artificially constructed code. Compare written dialogue with any transcript of an actual conversation, and you'll see that written language has entirely different conventions, rules, and structures than spoken language. The rules of this foreign language must be learned by the beginning writer—and they have to become second nature before the beginning writer can use written language to express ideas.

This is why so many young writers panic, freeze, weep, or announce that they hate to write. Try to put yourself in the position of the beginning writing student: Imagine that you've had a year or so of conversational French, taught in a traditional way out of a textbook, with practice in speaking twice a week or so. After that first year, your teacher asks you to explain the problem of evil in French. You're likely to experience brain freeze: a complete panic, a frantic scramble for words, a halting and incoherent attempt to express complicated ideas in a medium which is unfamiliar. Even another year or two of study won't make this kind of self-expression possible. Rather, the conventions of the French language need to become second nature, automatic—invisible to you—so that you can concentrate on the ideas, rather than on the medium used to express them.

The same is true for young writers. Ask a student to express ideas in writing before she is completely fluent in the rules and conventions of written language, and she'll freeze. She can't express her thoughts in writing, because she's still wrestling with the basic means of expression itself.

I have become convinced that most writing instruction is fundamentally flawed because children are never taught the most basic skill of writing, the skill on which everything rests: how to put words down on paper.

Writing is a process that involves two distinct mental steps. First, the writer puts an idea into words; then, she puts the words down on paper.

INARTICULATE IDEA ⟶ IDEA IN WORDS
IDEA IN WORDS ⟶ WORDS ON PAPER

Mature writers are able to do both steps without paying much attention to the fact that their brains are actually carrying out two different operations. But for the beginning writer, even a simple writing exercise ("Write down what you did this morning") requires the simultaneous performance of two new and difficult things. And so the student struggles—just as a baby who has barely learned to walk will struggle if you simultaneously ask him to perform some other task (such as rubbing his head). All of the baby's attention needs to go into moving his feet, until that action becomes automatic. If you ask him to walk and rub his head, he'll probably freeze in one place, swaying back and forth uncertainly—just like many new writers.

Young writers need time to learn the conventions of their new language. They need to become *fluent* in it before they can use it to express new ideas. But in most cases, students are simply immersed in this new language of writing. While immersion techniques often work for spoken foreign languages, they don't work nearly as well for writing—which is, after all, an artificial code rather than a natural speech expression.

Occasionally, this process produces a perfectly willing and competent writer—one who has a natural affinity for writing, and can intuitively grasp those parts of the process which have not been explicitly taught. But other students remain puzzled. They became frustrated and resistant, always struggling with the task of getting words on paper, never competent enough to let their ideas flow out.

Instead, the process of writing needs to be taught in an orderly, step-by-step method that will set young writers free to *use* their medium rather than wrestle with it.

The Three Stages

This book is a foundational text: it focuses on those all-important early years of writing. In these elementary years (roughly, grades one through four) the student masters the new and unfamiliar process of writing: putting ideas into words and putting those words down on paper.

He will begin by pulling apart the two steps of writing and practicing them separately. This is the essence of good teaching: breaking tasks down into their component elements and teaching students how to perform each element, before putting the elements back together. The pianist practices first the right hand, and then the left hand, before putting the two together; the young writer practices putting ideas into words, and then putting words down on paper, before trying to do both simultaneously.

Good writing requires *training*. It demands one-on-one attention. What follows will equip you to *train* the young student in the language of writing.

Writing with Ease (Years 1–4)

Elementary-school writing consists of copywork, dictation, and narration, all of which develop the student's basic skills with written language.

Years One and Two: Practicing Narration

Before requiring the student to write, teach him to *narrate*. Narration happens when the student takes something he's just read (or heard you read) and puts it into his own words.

This begins on a very simple level: You read to the student and ask him specific questions about what he's heard, such as "What was the most interesting thing in that story?" or "Who was that history lesson about?" You then require him to *answer you in complete sentences.* As the student grows more familiar with the process of narration, you can move on to more general questions such as "Summarize what we just read in your own words."

As the young student narrates out loud, he is practicing the first part of the writing process: putting an idea into his own words. He is practicing a new and difficult skill without having to come up with original ideas first; because his narrations are always rooted in content that he's just read or heard, he can concentrate on the task of expressing himself with words.

He is also practicing this new skill without having to worry about the *second* part of the writing process: putting those words down on paper. As he narrates, you—the teacher—write the words down for him as he watches. He can simply concentrate on the task at hand, without worrying about the mechanical difficulties of wielding a pencil. (For students whose fine motor skills are still developing, this is *essential*; they cannot focus on narration if they're also contemplating how much their hand is going to hurt when they have to write the narration down.)

Years One and Two: Copywork and Dictation

Separately, and preferably at a different time during the day, the student begins to master the second part of the process: putting words down on paper. This is not a simple task. It requires physical labor, fine motor coordination, and an understanding of the rules that govern written presentation: capitalization, punctuation, spacing, letter formation.

This skill is developed through copywork and dictation. Copywork and dictation allow the student to master the second step of the process without having to worry about the first, difficult task of putting ideas into words.

The beginning student doesn't even know yet how written language is supposed to look. Before he can put words down on paper, he must have some visual memory of what those words are supposed to look like. So during first grade, he'll copy out sentences from good writers, practicing the look and feel of properly written language.

Once the student has become accustomed to reproducing, on his own paper, properly written sentences placed in front of him as a model, you'll take the model away. Now that his mind is stocked with mental images of properly written language, he needs to learn how to visualize a written sentence in his mind and then put it down on paper.

From second grade on, rather than putting the written model in front of the student, you will dictate sentences to him. This will force him to bring his memory into play, to picture the sentence in his mind before writing it down. Eventually you'll be dictating two and three sentences at a time to a student, encouraging him to hold longer and longer chunks of text in his mind as he writes.

Many students who struggle with writing put down sentences that are lacking in punctuation, capitalization, or spacing—a clue that they have never learned to picture written language in their minds. Others can tell you with great fluency exactly what they want to write; if you then say to them, "Great! Write that down!" they'll ask, "What did I just say?" Both are clues that students have not learned to visualize sentences and hold them in mind—both essential if the student is ever going to get words down on paper. Moving from copywork to dictation develops these skills.

Years Three and Four: Putting the Two Steps Together

Around third grade, most students are ready to begin putting the two skills together. In third grade, students will begin to use part of their own narrations as dictation exercises. They will tell you the narration; you will write it down for them, and then dictate the first sentence back to them. Eventually they will learn that, in order to write, all they need to do is put an idea into words (something they've practiced extensively through narration), and then put those words down on paper (which they're accustomed to doing during dictation).

They will begin to write.

During the last two years of the elementary grades, you will concentrate on drawing the two skills together for the student. Some students will be able to bring the two steps together instinctively, without a struggle. But many need to be led through the process gradually, with plenty of practice, so that it can become second nature—and if they are not given this practice, they continue to struggle into middle school, high school, and beyond.

What You're Not Doing

But what about journaling, book reports, and imaginative writing?

In Years One through Four, it's not necessary for the student to do original writing. In fact, original writing (which requires not only a mastery of both steps of the writing process, but the ability to find something original to *say*) is beyond the developmental capability of many students.

There is plenty of time for original writing as the student's mind matures.

During the first four years, it is *essential* that students be allowed instead to concentrate on mastering the process: getting ideas into words, and getting those words down on paper.

Some children may be both anxious and willing to do original writing. This should never be discouraged. However, it should not be required either. Students who are required to write, write, write during elementary school are likely to produce abysmal compositions. Take the time to lay a foundation first; during the middle- and high-school years, the student can then build on it with confidence.

What Comes After the Fundamentals?

You're preparing your student to move into Years Five through Eight, the middle grades, when she'll learn how to put ideas in order; this in turn will prepare her for Years Nine throught Twelve, the high-school study of rhetoric (persuasive communication). Although you don't need to know what comes next in order to lay a strong foundation, I suggest that you read on so that you can gain an overview of the entire writing process.

Alternately, you can go directly to "Where Should I Begin?" on page 25, and start building that foundation right away.

Writing with Skill (Years 5–8)

In the middle grades the student learns to organize sentences into short compositions.

By now, he can put ideas he's already read into his own words and get those words down on paper without difficulty. The technical difficulty of learning the act of writing has been conquered. But until the student can begin to think about the *order* in which ideas should be set down, he'll continue to struggle with written composition. So during the middle-grade years, you'll help the student develop a toolbox of strategies for putting ideas into order.

Learning how to *order* ideas takes place on the microlevel (the sentence) and also on the macrolevel (the composition itself).

Diagramming: Sentence-Level Ordering

The primary tool that students will use to order ideas on the sentence level is diagramming. The middle-school student will learn to think critically about the structure of his sentences; he will use diagramming as a tool to fix weak sentences.

Weak sentences reveal problems in thinking.

A sentence which fits logically together is a sentence which is written in good style (poor style is most often the result of fuzzy thinking). Now that the student can get sentences down on paper, he needs to sharpen and focus them. Whenever a sentence doesn't "sound right" to him, he should examine the logical relationships between the parts of the sentence. Diagramming the sentence lays the logic of the sentence bare.

Consider the following balanced and beautiful sentence, from nineteenth-century poet Gerard Manley Hopkins: "Our prayer and God's grace are like two buckets in a well; while the one ascends, the other descends." Compare the sound of this sentence to a typical freshman composition thesis statement (this from an actual seminar paper I received several years ago from a student): "In *Pride and Prejudice,* her mother's bad manners and wishing to get married made Elizabeth discontent." While the second sentence makes sense, it's an ugly sentence—the kind that makes parents and teachers despair.

If the middle-grade student is able to diagram both sentences, she'll be able to see for herself why the first sentence resonates, while the second clunks.

In the Hopkins sentence, the subject and verb of the first independent clause are diagrammed like this:

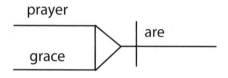

The second sentence also has a compound subject and single verb:

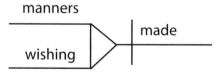

Although the second sentence is grammatically correct, it's ugly because the two subjects are two different kinds of words. "Manners" is a noun, while "wishing" is a gerund—a verb form *used* as a noun. Words which occupy parallel places on a diagram should take the same form—as in the Hopkins sentence, where "prayer" and "grace" are both nouns.

If the student sets out to fix the style problem in the second sentence, she'll also be forced to clarify her thinking. The noun "manners" represents something that Elizabeth's mother is doing *to* her; it's an outside circumstance. The verb form "wishing" is internal; it's Elizabeth's own action which is forcing her to be discontent. The two causes of her discontent aren't parallel. So what is the relationship between them? Do the mother's bad manners represent an entire social sphere from which Elizabeth longs to escape? Does she wish for a more genteel life, and does she wish to get married because that will allow her to move from one kind of life to another? Or is marriage itself Elizabeth's driving passion? Does she simply resent her mother's bad manners because they jeopardize her chances of attracting a bridegroom?

The middle-grade student won't necessarily understand all of this, but learning to diagram sentences will allow her to begin to understand the relationship between style and thought. Bad style is almost always a thinking problem, not a surface blemish.

For a slightly different illustration of this, consider the following sentence, also drawn from a freshman composition assignment, and containing a very common sort of beginning-writer error: "In addition to the city, Theodore Dreiser's society is depicted in its people."

This is the kind of sentence that *almost* makes sense; it's clear that the writer has an idea in mind, but that idea isn't coming through to the reader. But how can the student locate the problem?

Through diagramming. In this case, the subject (society) and verb (is depicted) are diagrammed on a simple subject/verb line, with the prepositional phrase "in

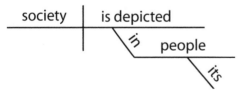

its people" diagrammed underneath the verb (it is acting as an adverb, because it answers the question "how"). But where should "In addition to the city" go?

It doesn't seem to fit anywhere. Are the society and city both depicted? (If so, what's the difference?) Is the society depicted in its people or in its city? (Neither is particularly clear.) The moral of this particular diagramming exercise: if you can't put it on the diagram, it doesn't belong in the sentence. The author of this sentence doesn't exactly know what Dreiser is depicting, and he's hoping to sneak his fuzzy comprehension past the reader.

One final example, this one slightly more subtle: "Therefore, the character of Irene is a summary of women of the time." This is a very common sort of beginner sentence: it makes sense, but it sounds immature. Why?

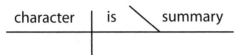

The tip-off to the problem is the slanting line, which indicates that the noun to the right is a predicate nominative. A predicate nominative must *rename* the subject. But "summary" is not another word for "character." The two are not even roughly parallel; a character can't be a summary any more than an elephant can be a mouse.

Diagramming teaches style, through clarifying the student's thought process; it begins to force the student to order ideas.

Outlining: Composition-Level Ordering

In this phase of the writing process, the student learns how to outline.

Writing programs suggest all different ways for students to brainstorm for ideas: drawing webs, free-writing, clustering, even making collages. But whatever brainstorming method the student uses, he cannot start writing until he knows in what order his ideas should be put down. He needs an entrance point, an orderly plan that will tell him: *First explain this idea; then explain how this and this relate to it; then move on to this observation.* Without such a plan, he will either panic, or wildly set down ideas in random order.

The student's ability to plan out and use an outline will not reach maturity until the high-school years. The middle-grade years are training years—a period of time in which the student learns the skills of outline-making.

This skill has two parts. First, the student needs to learn the technical skill of outlining: the correct form.

    I. MAIN POINT
      A. First supporting point
        1. Additional information about first supporting point
          a. Detail about that additional information

B. Second supporting point
    1. Additional information about that second supporting point
    2. More additional information about that second supporting point
II. NEXT MAIN POINT
III. NEXT MAIN POINT

and so forth.

Second, the student needs plenty of experience in outline construction.

The narration exercises of Year One allowed the student to order ideas naturally—chronologically, or possibly by putting the most interesting ideas first. But in Year Two, the student must develop one of the central skills in critical thinking: ranking information in order of importance, and figuring out the relationship between different assertions.

Outlining trains the mind in this skill. The most important assertions are marked I, II, III; the information that directly relates to those assertions is marked A, B, C; the facts that relate to *those* points are marked 1, 2, 3, and so on.

A well-planned composition should be outlined. But before asking students to outline their own original ideas, the thoughtful teacher gives them plenty of practice in outlining *other* writing. Careful educators never ask a student to do a task which has not first been modeled; a beginner can't do something that he has never seen done.

So between fifth and eighth grade, the student practices outlining pages from history and science (never fiction, which follows different rules). This skill should be developed slowly and carefully. In fifth grade, the student learns to pick out the central idea in each paragraph: the I, II, III, IV (and so on). In sixth grade, he learns to pick out the central idea along with one or two supporting facts. In seventh and eighth grade, he learns to pick out the central idea, the supporting facts, and additional details about the supporting facts.

In the early stages, while the student is learning to outline, she will continue to practice writing narrative summaries, using this now-familiar form as a platform to practice sentence style and structure. But by sixth and seventh grade, the narrative summaries will give way to a more advanced form of writing: writing from an outline.

After making an outline of a passage, the student will put the original away and then rewrite the passage, using only the outline. Then she'll compare her assignment with the original. Again, this is preparation for mature high-school writing; before the student is given the task of coming up with an outline and writing from it, she needs to see how *other* writers flesh out the bones of an outline.

What You're Still Not Doing

Up to this point, the student has not been required to do a great deal of original writing (although many students may choose to do so). But the student is nevertheless doing an enormous amount of writing practice: every day from first grade on, she's been either copying, taking dictation, writing down narrations, outlining, or writing from someone else's outline.

All of this practice is necessary so that the student can come up to the high-school start line equipped and ready to go, prepared to launch into the full-fledged study of rhetoric.

It's important to resist the my-child's-writing-more-than-your-child pressure. Your neighbor's seventh grader may be doing a big research paper, while your seventh grader is still outlining and rewriting. Don't fret. Those research papers have been thrown at that seventh grader without a great deal of preparation. He's probably struggling to figure out exactly what he's doing, making false start after false start, and ending up with a paper which is largely rehashed encyclopedia information. I've taught scores of students who went through classroom programs which had them doing book reports, research papers, and other long assignments as early as third grade. This doesn't improve writing skill; it just produces students who can churn out a certain number of pages, when required.

As someone who's had to read those pages, I can testify that this approach is not, across the board, working.

A decent research paper requires skills in outlining and in persuasive writing that fifth, sixth, and seventh graders have not yet developed. Instead, in fifth through eighth grade, students should be writing constant short compositions, developing necessary skills before being required to carry those skills through into an extended piece of work. They will begin to learn the skills of researching, documentation, and argumentation, but the full exercise of these skills will not take place for several more years.

In summary: in the middle grades, students should learn to diagram, outline, and then write from an outline. This is essential preparation for the high-school stage—the full-fledged study of rhetoric.

Writing with Style (Years 9–12)

In high school, the student—now fully equipped with the basic skills needed to produce an essay—begins to study rhetoric. He will use the tools of the *progymnasmata*, something which has almost fallen out of modern writing courses.

In ancient and medieval rhetoric, a certain set of exercises (beginning with such simple exercises as retelling a narrative in your own words, working up to more complex assignments such as proving an argument by supplying examples and analogies, or disproving an argument through reasoning) became standard among teachers of rhetoric. These exercises, known broadly as the progymnasmata ("preliminary exercises," because they preceded the mature exercise of rhetoric), were generally undertaken by older students, and in most cases young writers need a certain amount of time and maturity before they can benefit from the progymnasmata exercises. Now, however, students will begin original writing in earnest, and the progymnasmata exercises will give them the skills necessary to express their own ideas with grace and fluency.

The persuasive expression of ideas is the central focus in high-school writing. The ability to assert an opinion, and then to defend it with reason and rhetoric, is central to the teenager's sense of himself: until you know what you think and believe, and can explain *why* you believe it, you remain immature. "It is absurd," Aristotle declared, in his own treatise on rhetoric, "to hold that a man should be ashamed of inability to defend himself with his limbs, but not ashamed of an inability to defend himself with speech and reason; for the use of rational speech is more distinctive of a human being than the use of his limbs." In other words, articulate and persuasive speech is part of what *makes* us human.

So the rhetoric course should involve not just training in forms, but in words: What kinds of openings are best suited for different subjects? Is it more effective to write a series of short sentences, or several long ones with subordinated clauses? Should I appeal to analogy, use a metaphor, or avoid both? And many more considerations.

The Thesis Statement: Deciding What to Write About

Before the student can put the progymnasmata skills to work in writing, he must be able to come up with a thesis statement.

A thesis statement is a proposition you can defend, a statement you can prove or disprove, or an assertion that has to be supported by evidence. A thesis statement is not just a statement of fact. In most cases, the first topical statement a student comes up with when he decides to write is a statement of fact, not an assertion that can be proved.

> **Homer and William Blake both talk about nature.**
> **Jane Austen's characters can't be open about their feelings.**
> **Hamlet had a fatal flaw.**

All of these are statements of fact, not thesis statements. Yes, Homer and William Blake both talk about nature; this is an observation that can be proved true with a single glance at each. Yes, Jane Austen's characters can't be open about their feelings; this is right on the surface of every character interaction. Of course Hamlet had a fatal flaw; that's why he (and practically everyone else) dies. A paper that begins with a statement of fact can only go in one direction: listing examples, something which rapidly becomes very boring indeed.

There is, of course, a place for developing statements of fact: the traditional research paper. The high-school student will learn to produce these papers, but he'll find that college writing (and mature adult writing after education ends) tends to reward skills in persuasive writing—despite the fact that the research paper is often the capstone of high-school writing programs.

In order to write a persuasive composition, students need to be able to take that initial statement of fact and turn it into a thesis statement. Beginning thesis-writers can use three questions that will help guide them from the opening statement towards the formulation of a thesis.

The first question: How are these things the same, and how are they different? Blake and Homer both talk about nature, which is the obvious similarity between the two. But what's the difference? *Homer sees nature as a hostile force to be reckoned with while Blake sees nature as a friend of man.* This assumes the fact (that they both talk about nature) but then makes an assertion about it: the two men treat nature differently. This kind of paper—the comparison/contrast paper—is often the best place for a beginner to start.

The second question: Why? In *Pride and Prejudice, Elizabeth pretends to conceal her feelings, but she actually reveals them to Mr. Darcy in many subtle ways.* It's a given that Elizabeth can't be open about her feelings, the question is *why?* In her case, she is restricted by the polite society around her, forced to find more indirect ways of showing her emotions.

The third question: When? *Hamlet is sane throughout most of the play, but goes mad during the duel.* This assertion argues that there's a transition point in the play where Hamlet moves into insanity—something that the writer will now have to prove by analyzing Hamlet's speeches and actions.

The Progymnasmata: Techniques of Persuasion

The high-school years are the time for students to study the techniques of effective persuasion. During Years Nine through Twelve, the high-school student will progress through a systematic study of the progymnasmata: among other skills, these teach writing a variety of narratives (condensed, amplified, biographical, and more), using different modes of narrative (direct, indirect, interrogative, comparative), mastering the art of description, learning how to use such sentence-level strategies as parallelism, parataxis, and multiple coordination, supporting arguments through reasoning and anecdote, using dialogue, and much more.

As part of the progymnasmata exercises, the student will analyze different kinds of writing, outlining them and becoming familiar with their forms. This will involve some rewriting from outlines, as in the middle grades, but the purpose of *this* rewriting is not to learn how to outline, but rather to develop knowledge of different styles and methods of argumentation.

Constant Short Papers

Throughout the high-school years, as he works through the progymnasmata, the student should write three to five one-page papers per week, taking his topics from literature, history, science, and his other high-school courses. Every time the student has to complete a one-page paper, he has to go through the process of formulating a thesis statement, deciding on a form and a strategy, constructing an outline, and writing from it. This constant repetition is much more valuable than two or three long writing projects undertaken over the course of the year.

In the last two years of high school, students should *also* pursue those longer projects, completing at least two lengthy research-style papers on a topic of their own choosing. These longer papers make use of the skills developed by the short papers, and also stretch the student towards a more detailed and complex form.

Rather than rushing to push children into more mature tasks, the twelve-level progression I've outlined takes the time and trouble to *prepare* students for writing. The goal is to turn the young writer into a thoughtful student who can *make use* of written language, rather than struggle with it.

Using This Book

Writing with Ease: Strong Fundamentals will take you through the step-by-step process of teaching young students to write, over the course of four carefully graded levels of assignments. Each level is designed to be completed in a single school year of 36 weeks, although many students will move more quickly and some will need to progress at a slightly slower pace.

For each step in the process, I have provided a week of complete, scripted lessons, including reading passages and narration and copywork assignments. You can then choose to continue to work on the skills described by selecting your own reading, narration, and copywork assignments from the student's history, science, and literature books, or from your own favorite texts. Parents and teachers who have strong opinions about the topics they prefer students to cover may wish to take this route.

However, you can also make use of the workbooks published by Peace Hill Press. These workbooks contain, in worksheet form, the scripted lessons laid out in this text; they also contain fully developed lessons for all 36 weeks of the school year, including copywork worksheets, dictation instructions and worksheets, reading passages, comprehension questions, and sample narrations. Although these workbooks are not necessary to complete *Writing with Ease*, they are designed to help you spend your time teaching, rather than searching for source materials.

For more information on the workbooks, go to www.peacehillpress.com.

Year One
First Grade or Level One

Year One, Weeks 1–3

Copywork sentences are around four to eight words; beginning narration exercises are practiced on two-paragraph readings.

Year One, Weeks 4–10

Copywork sentences remain essentially the same length, but introduce proper names. Narration exercises grow a little longer. The student begins to use his own narration sentences for copywork; this is the first step towards writing original sentences.

Year One, Weeks 11–19

Copywork sentences grow slightly longer; additional proper names are introduced, as well as pronouns. Narration exercises consist of three longer paragraphs. The student continues to use his own sentences for copywork.

Year One, Weeks 20–27

Copywork sentences lengthen again and introduce abbreviations, titles of respect, the seasons, and proper usage. Narrations lengthen as well. The student continues to use his own sentences for copywork.

Year One, Weeks 28–35

Copywork sentences lengthen once more and introduce proper poetic form and a variety of ending punctuation marks. Narrations also become more complex. The student continues to use his own sentences for copywork.

Year One Mastery Evaluation, Week 36

Year Two
Second Grade or Level Two

Year Two, Weeks 1–10

The student begins dictation by first copying a sentence of ten to twelve words, and then taking the sentence from dictation on another day; the sentences introduce action and linking verbs, the four sentence types, and comma use. Narration passages begin at around four paragraphs; after answering comprehension questions, the student identifies the most important element of the passage. Narration sentences are used for dictation after the student examines them.

Year Two, Weeks 11–18

Copywork sentences are still used for dictation, but their length grows to 12 to 15 words; the sentences introduce helping verbs, contractions, adjectives, interjections, conjunctions, and direct quotations. Narration passages expand slightly in length; narration sentences are used for dictation, but the student does not examine them first.

Year Two, Weeks 19–27

Copywork sentences are still used for dictation; dialogue and multiple sentences are introduced. Narration passages remain the same length; narration sentences are used for dictation, but the student does not examine them first.

Year Two, Weeks 28–35

Dictation sentences of 12 to15 words *replace* copywork; articles, prepositions, synonyms, and antonyms are emphasized. Narration passages increase in length; the student is encouraged to answer the more general "Can you give me a short summary of this passage?" Narration sentences are used for dictation, but the student does not examine them first.

Year Two Mastery Evaluation, Week 36

Year Three
Third Grade or Level Three

Year Three, Weeks 1–10

Narration exercises remain around six paragraphs, but the student reads the passage independently before answering comprehension questions; he then summarizes the passage in two or three short sentences. Dictation sentences remain at 12 to15 words, alternating one long and two short sentences; narration sentences are used for dictation.

Year Three, Weeks 11–19

Narration exercises remain around the same length. The student reads the passage independently before answering comprehension questions and providing a brief summary. Dictation exercises lengthen to 15 to 18 words of two sentences, taken down after three repetitions; two narration sentences are used for dictation.

Year Three, Weeks 20–27

Narration exercises remain the same length, but the student narrates without first answering comprehension questions. Dictation exercises lengthen to 16 to 20 words of two longer or three shorter sentences, taken down after three repetitions; two narration sentences are used for dictation.

Year Three, Weeks 28–35

Narration exercises lengthen. Dictation exercises remain at 16 to 20 words, two longer or three shorter sentences, taken down after three repetitions. The student repeats one sentence of his narration to himself and takes the sentence down from his own dictation.

Year Three Mastery Evaluation, Week 36

Year Four
Fourth Grade or Level Four

Year Four, Weeks 1–10

Narration exercises lengthen to eight to ten paragraphs; the student continues to respond to directed narration starters. Dictation exercises remain at approximately 20 words, two longer or three shorter sentences, taken down after three repetitions. The student repeats one sentence of his narration to himself and takes the sentence down from his own dictation.

Year Four, Weeks 11–19

Narration exercises remain at around the same length. Dictation exercises remain at around 20 words, but introduce proper paragraph form. The student repeats two narration sentences to himself and takes the sentences down from his own dictation.

Year Four, Weeks 20–27

Narration exercises lengthen slightly. Dictation exercises lengthen to 25- to 30-word paragraphs, repeated three times. The student repeats two narration sentences to himself and takes the sentences down from his own dictation.

Year Four, Weeks 28–35

Narration exercises remain at the same length; after reading the passage independently, the student answers the general question "What is this passage about?" rather than relying on directed narration starters. Dictation exercises remain 25- 30-word paragraphs, repeated three times. The student writes his own narration in proper paragraph form.

Year Four Mastery Evaluation, Week 36

Where Should I Begin?

If you're beginning this program with a preschooler, you can simply start with the prewriting exercises; for a first grader, start with Year One. Progress forward at whatever pace seems comfortable for the child. With an older student, however, you'll need to evaluate your student's current writing level in order to decide where to begin.

Each of the levels that follow concludes with an evaluation lesson. Choose the evaluation lesson that corresponds to your student's grade level, and work through it together.

Grade One	Year One Mastery Evaluation, p. 66
Grade Two	Year Two Mastery Evaluation, p. 108
Grade Three	Year Three Mastery Evaluation, p. 155
Grade Four	Year Four Mastery Evaluation, p. 215

If the student is able to do the evaluation without a struggle, go ahead and begin the next level (so, for example, a second grader who finished the Year Two evaluation without trouble should start with the first lesson of Year Three).

However, if the student is unable to finish the evaluation assignment successfully, begin at the start of that level and work forwards. If you find him struggling with the lessons, go back to the *previous* level and complete that level first. Remember: you can progress through the levels at whatever speed is natural to the student. It is always better to start with too-simple material and move quickly through it, than to begin with skills that are slightly too difficult.

You may find that a reluctant writer ends up back in Year Two or Three—even if the student is older. Don't be afraid to go back and do this early work before moving on. Writing is a sequential skill. The student *must* know how to put an idea in words and how to put words down on paper before he can move on to outlining; the student must know how to outline and plan before he can move on to full-fledged rhetoric. A reluctant writer is generally reluctant because, somewhere along the line, she's missed one of those steps. You must go back and build the basic skills before the student can progress forwards; simply assigning more and more complicated writing tasks will result in greater and greater frustration.

Can an older student profit from this book?

If you have a reluctant older writer—anywhere between fifth and twelfth grade—try the following diagnostic tests.

First, ask the student to tell you what he wants to write. (Assure him that he won't have to write the words down; you want to find out whether he is able to complete the first part of the writing process, the task of putting ideas into words.) If he is unable to put his ideas into coherent, complete sentences, he has never learned how to assemble his ideas into a form which can even be put down on paper. This student should begin with the narration exercises in Year One, and should continue through them until he is able to answer the question "What was that passage about?" with three or four fluent, complete sentences (a goal reached by the end of Year Four).

Second, dictate two sentences to the student. Tell the student that you will read the two sentences three times, and that the student should then write the sentences down. If the student can do this without effort, there is no need to do either the copywork or dictation exercises in this book—although the student may still need practice in narration.

However, you may find that the student runs into one of two difficulties. He may put down a misspelled, wrongly punctuated version of the sentences. This demonstrates that the student has never learned how to picture written language properly in his head; he has no visual memory of correctly written sentences. This student will probably need to go all the way back to Year One and do some copywork before moving on to dictation, and should continue on through the dictation exercises of Year Four.

Second, you may find that the student is unable to remember the sentences long enough to put them down on paper. This too represents a writing problem. This is the kind of the student who is often able to tell you fluently what he wants to write, but when you then say, "Great! Write that down!" asks, "What did I say?" He is unable to hold sentences in his head while he writes—and until he is able to do this, he will remain frustrated. This student need not go back to copywork, but should begin with the dictation exercises in Year Two and work all the way up through Year Four.

Finally, you may find that your student can tell you what he wants to write, and can take dictation, but struggles to get words down on paper anyway. For some reason, the student is unable to complete the process of writing.

This student probably doesn't need to do the exercises in *Writing with Ease* at all; he's almost ready to begin a writing program that focuses on the organization of ideas. To prepare him fully for the next stage of writing—the stage in which he will learn to analyze and organize his thoughts—give him some practice in "dictating" to himself. Ask the student to tell a tape recorder what he wants to write, and then to play the tape back and take dictation from it. He may need to do this for some months, but eventually he'll realize that he doesn't need the tape recorder; he can simply tell himself what he wants to write, and then put the words down from his own mental "dictation."

PART II

THE LESSONS

Preschool and Kindergarten

I f your young child is reading words of four or more letters, has learned how to form all of her handwritten letters and can do so without frustration, and can concentrate on a task for ten minutes or more, you can skip this prewriting section and go directly to Year One, although you may find it helpful to read through the information in this section for tips on building language-arts skills.

However, I do not encourage parents to push children into first-grade writing skills early; it's often much better to take advantage of a late birthday and allow the child an additional year to mature. If your child is younger than six, don't feel that you're gaining some kind of advantage by beginning Year One work early. Work on handwriting skills, work on phonics skills, do the prewriting level of this program, and read, read, read together. Wait until the child is first-grade age before starting on the Year One exercises.

Overview of the Early Years: How to Teach Informally

In the years before formal schooling begins, there is no need to do a prepared curriculum. In fact, I find that most kindergarten language-arts curricula are totally unnecessary. On the first day of school, your first-grade student should know how to form his letters and numbers and how to sound out simple three- and four-letter words. If he can progress a little faster in reading and begin first-grade reading on a higher level, he'll have an advantage; but this is not necessary.

However, there are some informal teaching techniques that you can use to give your child a jump start.

Teaching through Conversation

When the child begins first-grade writing, one of his first challenges will be to take inarticulate ideas and put them into complete sentences. He'll have to be able to do this before he can begin to write.

So help him prepare by speaking to him in complete sentences whenever possible, and encouraging him to speak in complete sentences as well. Start out by listening to yourself: is most of your conversation with the child phrases and fragments? (Stop! No. Sure, why not. OK. Is that because? Oh, you're going to. Here.) When you listen carefully, you'll be surprised how easy it is to fall into a pattern of only speaking to a young child in partial sentences. But when you take the effort to speak to a child in complete sentences, you are modeling the skill of taking an idea and putting it into words.

Turning Fragments into Complete Sentences

The first technique to master is that of taking the child's fragments and repeating them back to him as complete sentences. Young children naturally speak in words and phrases; you need to model more complex sentences. When you speak to the child, listen for his answer and repeat it; then repeat it again, this time as a complete sentence.

> **Parent:** Which shoes do you want to wear?
> **Child:** *Those.*
> **Parent:** You would like to wear those pink sneakers?

> **Parent:** What book should we read?
> **Child:** Frog and Toad.
> **Parent:** We'll read the book called *Frog and Toad* together.

> **Child:** *Cookie.*
> **Parent:** Would you like to have a cookie? Here is a cookie. (Or, You can have a cookie after dinner, but not right now. Have a piece of celery instead.)

> **Child:** *Where's Blankie?*
> **Parent:** Do you need to find your blankie? Let's look for the blankie together. Maybe your blankie is underneath your bed.

Saying Sentences with and without Contractions

Try to develop the habit of saying sentences with and without contractions. Listen to yourself; whenever you use a contraction, repeat the sentence again without the contraction.

> **Parent:** Don't touch the stove; it's hot. Do not touch the stove; it is hot.

> **Parent:** I didn't hear you. I did not hear you.

> **Parent:** I'll come tuck you in soon. I will come tuck you in soon.

Talking as You Work

Remind yourself to talk while you work around the house: to tell the child what you're doing as you do it. This teaches the child that language is used to describe; it also models proper ordering of ideas.

> **Parent:** I'm going to make spaghetti for dinner. First I'm going to put water in this big pot. I'll put some salt in the water too. Now I'm putting the pot on the stove and turning the burner on. Now I'm waiting for the water to boil. After the water boils, I'll break up the spaghetti and drop it in.

> **Parent:** I need to look up a telephone number. I don't know the name of the store, so I'm going to use the Yellow Pages. I know it's an appliance store, so I'll look under A for Appliance. Look at all of those ads for appliance stores! The store I want to find is in Madison Heights. This must be it—the address says Madison Heights. It doesn't open until 9 AM, so I'll have to wait half an hour before I call.

Using Audiobooks to Develop Language Skills

Play audiobooks (unabridged) for the child in the car, around the house, and during rest time. Even toddlers can enjoy listening to children's books on tape or CD.

Written language is different than spoken language. Allowing a child to listen to audiobooks begins to get the structure of written language into the child's mind. It also familiarizes the child with written language which is on a more difficult level than the child is able to read. When the child encounters written language, it will resonate; he's already been exposed to it. When he begins to write, his mind and ear will be well stocked with the structures of phrases, verbs, nouns, and so on. Audiobooks prepare a child both to read and to write.

Teaching Letter Recognition

Although this book deals primarily with writing, reading and writing are two facets of the same language skill. Before a child can write, he must be able to recognize and sound out his letters. Prepare young children for reading in the following ways:

Teach toddlers the alphabet song by singing it to them from the time that they are babies.

Teach letter recognition—not in formal sessions, but throughout the day. Put an alphabet chart somewhere in the child's room, with both upper- and lowercase letters on it. From the beginning, tell the child that each letter has both a name and a sound. If a child can learn that a cat says "meow," he can also learn that a letter called "b" makes the sound "b, b, b." (For this purpose, you'll choose one sound for each letter. The child will learn, for example, that "a" makes the short sound "a" as in "cat"; later, he'll learn that sometimes "a" has other sounds.)

Reinforce letter learning by playing letter games with the child. Put lower- and uppercase magnet letters on the refrigerator. Start with two letters which look quite different from each other (for a total of four—an upper- and lowercase D and an upper- and lowercase E, for example). Put those four letters on the refrigerator. Ask the child to bring you "a big D" or "a small e" or some other letter. Help him find the letter; praise him when he brings you the letter. When he can bring you the letter you ask for every time, add another lower- and uppercase letter. Gradually work up to the entire alphabet.

Beginning Handwriting

As soon as the child begins to show an interest in holding a pencil or crayon, make sure that the child holds the pencil properly. The classic pencil grip is the one which causes the least stress and strain on the young hand muscles.

If necessary, purchase rubber pencil grips and place

them on every pencil in the house that the child uses in order to ensure the proper grip.

Encourage children, even when scribbling, to draw circles and loops counterclockwise, not clockwise. Most handwriting curves are written counterclockwise; for some reason, however, the natural tendency of children is to draw circles clockwise. Show the child how to draw snowmen, slinkies, smoke from a train, car wheels, and other circles and spirals, by beginning at the upper right hand of the circle and moving counterclockwise.

When the child begins to try to form letters on his own (or in the K5 year, whichever comes earlier), begin a formal handwriting program. There's no need to do this for more than five minutes a day, at the start; short frequent repetitions will build the child's skill without tiring his hand or frustrating him.

Teaching Reading

Reading specialist Jessie Wise (my mother) likes to say, "'Better late than early' is a good principle for sending the child into a classroom setting, but 'Better early than late' is a good philosophy for teaching children to read." When your child turns five (earlier if the child shows an interest), try doing very basic and beginning phonics for five minutes per day. Aim to work up to a ten-minute lesson by the middle of the K5 year, and to a twenty-minute lesson by the end of the year.

Remember these three key words:

> **PATIENCE.** Don't get exasperated when the child doesn't remember. Never say, "We've been over this and over this. What do you mean, you don't remember?" Just tell the child the sound of the problem letter and move on.

> **FREQUENCY.** Five or ten minutes twice a day is more useful than twenty minutes at a stretch. Repeat daily for short periods; review often.

> **CONSISTENCY.** Don't take long periods off; children forget. At the beginning of phonics learning, try not to take more than a weekend or so off at a time. As the child grows more practiced, taking a week or more off for a family vacation or holiday won't do any harm. But never take months away from reading; the child will remember nothing.

When you begin reading with a small child, watch out for programs that tie reading and writing together by having the child learn to write sounds as she learns to sound them out. Many children are ready to read long before their fine motor skills are developed; asking them to write as they learn to read (as many phonics programs do, in part because a number of the better programs were originally developed for remedial use with older students) can frustrate them with the whole project. Instead, look for a program that will allow you to sit on the sofa with the child and learn the sounds and combinations.

Moving on to Year One

It is perfectly normal for six-year-olds to still be working through the basics of phonics. Simply continue on consistently, regularly, and patiently. Do not begin Year One of this program until the student can read four-letter words (consonant blends and vowel combinations).

It is also normal for children to struggle with the mechanical act of writing; this does not symbolize a learning difficulty (particularly for boys). However, if a child still complains of hand pain or has difficulty forming letters at the age of seven, you might consider checking with an educational specialist to see whether the child's fine motor skills can be improved through exercises or therapy.

Children who are reversing letters when they write are perfectly ready to move on to Year One. Reversal of letters is normal for young students; it does not signify dyslexia unless it persists well into later grammar school (and some children may reverse certain letters, such as "b" and "d," even longer). However, if the child reverses *all* letters or seems unable to recognize a letter when looking at it, consider checking with an educational specialist.

Students who struggle with reading and writing should always have their sight checked.

Year One
First Grade (or Level One, for Older Writers)

In Year One, the student begins to lay the foundation for good upper-level writing. She will work on the two most basic skills of writing (taking thoughts and putting them into words, and then taking words and putting them down on paper) separately, until both skills are fully mastered.

The first skill (taking thoughts and putting them into words) is practiced through narration. In Year One, the student will practice putting thoughts into complete sentences which are ready to be set down on paper. She will listen to a passage, answer questions about it as a way of preparing her to come up with a sentence of her own, and then express an idea about the passage in a complete sentence, ready to be written down. You will then write this sentence as she watches, modeling the completed process for her.

The second skill (taking words and putting them down on paper) is practiced through copywork. For all of Year One, the student will work on reproducing written models that introduce her to a sequence of written skills: punctuation, capitalization, and proper sentence styles.

The lessons that follow spell out an entire week's assignments whenever the student progresses from one step to the next. If you wish, you can then follow the pattern of this model work, but choose your own copywork and narration assignments. Alternatively, you can use the Year One workbook; this provides a full sequence of copywork and narration assignments that introduce the student sequentially to the necessary grammatical elements.

Year One, Weeks 1–3

The student begins with very brief copywork sentences of four to eight words, practicing capitalization and end punctuation marks. The beginning narration exercises allow the student to practice recollection and speaking in complete sentences; these exercises are short as well, around two paragraphs.

Week 1 spells out these developments; Weeks 2 and 3 are modeled on the Week 1 pattern.

WEEK 1

DAY ONE: The First Copywork Exercise

When the student first begins copywork, be sure to sit with him as he copies. Although it seems natural to you to reproduce the capitalization and punctuation in the model, the student hasn't yet learned to notice the proper form of written language. If he begins to write the first letter as a small letter, stop him before he finishes the letter and remind him of the rule: "What does a sentence begin with? A capital letter." If he forgets to leave a space between words, remind him to use his finger as a spacer; if he ignores the punctuation at the end of the sentence, say, "What does a sentence end with? A punctuation mark. What kind of punctuation mark is that?" Never allow the student to write incorrectly; the whole purpose of the exercise is to accustom him to the look of *correct* written language. And since the physical act of writing is so difficult for young students, always allow him to erase and correct; never require him to recopy.

Copy out one of the following sentences on first-grade lined paper, in neat print handwriting, for the student to copy. Choose whichever length is appropriate to the student's handwriting ability.

Explain to the student that these sentences are from the first chapter of *Little House in the Big Woods*, by Laura Ingalls Wilder. *Little House* is about a family that lives in Wisconsin in the 1860s, in a deep forest where few others live.

There were no roads.

The deer and the rabbits would be shy and swift.

Ask the student to copy the sentence in pencil on the line below the model. Point out to the student that this is a complete sentence; it begins with a capital letter and ends with a period.

DAY TWO: The First Narration Exercise

When doing the first narration exercise, remember that the goal is to teach the student to express herself in complete sentences. If she answers you in fragments, repeat the answer back to her in a complete sentence, and then have her repeat that sentence after you. If the student can't answer the question, read the part of the passage that contains the answer and then ask the question again.

When all of the questions have been answered, ask the student, "What is one thing that you remember about the passage?" If the student cannot answer you, ask one of the questions again, and take the answer as the narration.

If she answers in several sentences, ask her which of those sentences is the most important. Distinguishing between central facts and details is a skill which will be fully developed in the second phase of writing (Years 5–8, roughly corresponding to middle school and junior high). But it is important for the student to begin now to learn how to pick important facts out of a passage, rather than simply repeating all of the information.

Read the following passage to the student:

> Once upon a time, sixty years ago, a little girl lived in the Big Woods of Wisconsin, in a little gray house made of logs.
>
> The great, dark trees of the Big Woods stood all around the house, and beyond them were other trees and beyond them were more trees. As far as a man could go to the north in a day, or a week, or a whole month, there was nothing but woods. There were no houses. There were no roads. There were no people. There were only trees and the wild animals who had their homes among them.
>
> —From *Little House in the Big Woods*
> by Laura Ingalls Wilder

Ask the following questions:

Instructor: How many years ago does this story happen?
Student: *This story happens sixty years ago.*
(If necessary, you can explain to the student that this book was written in the 1920s. When Laura Ingalls Wilder was writing this first chapter, her childhood in the 1860s was sixty years ago. Now, we would say that the story happened almost 150 years ago!)

Instructor: Where did the little girl live?
Student: *She lived in Wisconsin OR in the big woods of Wisconsin.*

Instructor: If a man went north for a whole month, what would he find?
Student: *He would find more woods.*

Instructor: There were no roads in the Big Woods. Can you remember two other things that the Big Woods did not have?
Student: *There were no houses. There were no people.*

Instructor: Who *did* live among the trees?
Student: *Wild animals lived among the trees.*

Ask, "What is one thing you remember about the passage?" Write the student's answer down on first-grade lined paper as he watches. This answer can be the same as one of the answers above.

DAY THREE: Copywork

Copy out one of the following sentences on first-grade lined paper, in neat print handwriting, for the student to copy. Choose whichever length is appropriate to the student's handwriting ability. Both of these sentences are also from *Little House in the Big Woods.*

Pa owned a pig.

There was plenty of fresh meat to last for a long time.

Ask the student to copy the sentence in pencil on the line below the model. Point out to the student that this is a complete sentence; it begins with a capital letter and ends with a period.

DAY FOUR: Narration Exercise

Read the following passage to the student. Explain that the Ingalls family needed the pig so that they would have meat to eat in the winter; since there were no grocery stores, Pa had to raise the pig for food.

> Once in the middle of the night Laura woke up and heard the pig squealing. Pa jumped out of bed, snatched his gun from the wall, and ran outdoors. Then Laura heard the gun go off once, twice.
>
> When Pa came back, he told what had happened. He had seen a big black bear standing beside the pigpen. The bear was reaching into the pen to grab the pig, and the pig was running and squealing. Pa saw this in the starlight and he fired quickly. But the light was dim and in his haste he missed the bear. The bear ran away into the woods, not hurt at all.

—From *Little House in the Big Woods*
by Laura Ingalls Wilder

Ask the following questions:

Instructor: What did Laura hear when she woke up?
Student: *She heard the pig squealing.*

Instructor: What did Pa do when he heard the pig squeal?
Student: *He got his gun and went outside.*

Instructor: How many times did the gun go off?
Student: *It went off twice.*

Instructor: What did Pa see when he went outside?
Student: *He saw a black bear standing beside the pigpen.*

Instructor: What was the bear trying to do?

Student: *It was trying to grab the pig.*

Instructor: When Pa shot at the bear, he missed because he was in a hurry. What is the other reason that he missed the bear?
Student: *The light was dim.*

Ask, "What is one thing you remember about the passage?" Write the student's answer down on first-grade lined paper as he watches.

WEEKS 2–3

Follow the same weekly pattern as above:

DAY ONE: Copywork

DAY TWO: Narration Exercise

DAY THREE: Copywork

DAY FOUR: Narration Exercise

Choose sentences of five to eight words and narrations of around two paragraphs from the student's history, science, and literature books.

Over these two weeks, look for copywork sentences that contain the first names of particular people. Explain to the student that these are called "proper names" and should begin with a capital letter. Make sure that the student copies the proper names correctly. If the student randomly capitalizes other words, remind her to capitalize only the proper names as well as the first word in the sentence.

Year One, Weeks 4–10

In Weeks 4 through 10, copywork sentences remain essentially the same length, while introducing a variety of proper names. Narration exercises grow a little longer, helping to develop the student's memory and retention.

The student will also begin to use her own narration sentences for copywork, the first step in learning to write original sentences.

Week 4 spells out these developments; Weeks 5 through 10 are modeled on the Week 4 pattern.

WEEK 4

DAY ONE: Copywork

Copy out one of the following sentences on first-grade lined paper, in neat print handwriting, for the student to copy. Choose whichever length is appropriate to the student's handwriting ability.

Explain to the student that these sentences are from *Alice's Adventures in Wonderland*, by Lewis Carroll. Alice has fallen down a rabbit-hole, and now she is wandering through a very strange country. In this country, she is only three inches tall—and she has just met a large blue caterpillar who is sitting on top of a mushroom.

Alice was silent.

The caterpillar was the first to speak.

DAY TWO: Narration Exercise

Explain to the student that a "hookah" is an old-fashioned type of pipe, and that to "contradict" someone is to say the opposite of what they tell you.

> The Caterpillar was the first to speak.
> "What size do you want to be?" it asked.
> "Oh, I'm not particular as to size," Alice hastily replied;
> "Only one doesn't like changing so often, you know."
> "I *don't* know," said the Caterpillar.
> Alice said nothing: she had never been so much
> contradicted in all her life before, and she felt that she was

losing her temper.

"Are you content now?" said the Caterpillar.

"Well, I should like to be a *little* larger, sir, if you wouldn't mind," said Alice: "three inches is such a wretched height to be."

"It is a very good height indeed!" said the Caterpillar angrily, rearing itself upright as it spoke (it was exactly three inches high).

"But I'm not used to it!" pleaded poor Alice in a piteous tone. And she thought to herself, "I wish the creatures wouldn't be so easily offended!"

"You'll get used to it in time," said the Caterpillar; and it put the hookah into its mouth and began smoking again.

This time Alice waited patiently until it chose to speak again. In a minute or two the Caterpillar took the hookah out of its mouth and yawned once or twice, and shook itself. Then it got down off the mushroom, and crawled away into the grass merely remarking as it went, "One side will make you grow taller, and the other side will make you grow shorter."

"One side of *what?* The other side of *what?* " thought Alice to herself.

"Of the mushroom," said the Caterpillar, just as if she had asked it aloud; and in another moment it was out of sight.

—From *Alice's Adventures in Wonderland*
by Lewis Carroll

Ask the following questions:

Instructor: How tall is the Caterpillar?
Student: He is three inches tall.

Instructor: Does Alice like being three inches tall?
Student: No, she doesn't.

Instructor: Does she want to be smaller or larger?
Student: She wants to be larger.

Instructor: What does the Caterpillar tell Alice, right before he crawls away?
Student: He says, "One side will make you taller and the other will make you shorter."

Instructor: What is he talking about?
Student: He is talking about the mushroom.

Ask, "What is one thing you remember about the passage?" Write the student's answer down on first-grade lined paper as he watches.

DAY THREE: Copywork
Copy out one of the following sentences on first-grade lined paper, in neat print handwriting, for the student to copy. Choose whichever length is appropriate to the student's handwriting ability.

Explain to the student that, at the end of *Alice's Adventures in Wonderland*, Alice goes to the trial of the Knave of Hearts, who is accused of stealing a plate of tarts (which are like tiny pies) from the Queen of Hearts. There are twelve "jurors" at the trial—animals who will listen to the evidence and decide whether the Knave of Hearts is guilty.

The first witness was the Hatter.

One of the jurors had a pencil that squeaked.

DAY FOUR: Narration Exercise and Copywork

The King and Queen of Hearts were seated on their throne when they arrived, with a great crowd assembled about them—all sorts of little birds and beasts, as well as the whole pack of cards: the Knave was standing before them, in chains, with a soldier on each side to guard him; and near the King was the White Rabbit, with a trumpet in one hand, and a scroll of parchment in the other. In the very middle of the court was a table, with a large dish of tarts upon it: they looked so good, that it made Alice quite hungry to look at them—"I wish they'd get the trial done," she thought, "and hand round the

year one – week 4

refreshments!" But there seemed to be no chance of this, so she began looking about her, to pass away the time.

Alice had never been in a court of justice before, but she had read about them in books, and she was quite pleased to find that she knew the name of nearly everything there. "That's the judge," she said to herself, "because of his great wig." The judge, by the way, was the King; and as he wore his crown over the wig...he did not look at all comfortable, and it was certainly not becoming.

"And that's the jury-box," thought Alice, "and those twelve creatures" (she was obliged to say "creatures," you see, because some of them were animals, and some were birds), "I suppose they are the jurors." She said this last word two or three times over to herself, being rather proud of it: for she thought, and rightly too, that very few little girls of her age knew the meaning of it at all. However, "jurymen" would have done just as well.

—From *Alice's Adventures in Wonderland*
by Lewis Carroll

Ask the following questions:

Instructor: Besides Alice, can you name two other characters who were in the part of the story I just read?
Student: The King and Queen of Hearts, the Knave of Hearts, and the White Rabbit were all in the story.

Instructor: What was on the table in the very middle of the court?
Student: There was a large dish of tarts on the table.

Instructor: What was the judge wearing that helped Alice recognize him?
Student: He was wearing a wig.

Instructor: Who was the judge?
Student: The judge was the King of Hearts.

Instructor: Who were the jurors?
Student: *The jurors were animals and birds.*

Instructor: Why was Alice proud of knowing the word "juror"?
Student: *She thought that few little girls her age would know that word.*

Ask, "What is one thing you remember about the passage?" Write the student's answer down on first-grade lined paper as he watches.

Place this written answer in front of the student. Ask him to copy the sentence in pencil on the line below the model. If the sentence is too long for comfort, he can copy only the first six to eight words.

WEEKS 5–10

Follow the same weekly pattern as above:

DAY ONE: Copywork

DAY TWO: Narration Exercise

DAY THREE: Copywork

DAY FOUR: Narration Exercise and Copywork

Choose sentences of five to eight words and narrations of approximately three short paragraphs from the student's history, science, and literature books.

Over these six weeks, look for copywork sentences that contain the proper names of people, cities, and states. Explain to the student that these are called "proper names" and should begin with a capital letter. Make sure that the student copies the proper names correctly. If the student randomly capitalizes other words, remind her to capitalize only the proper names as well as the first word in the sentence.

Introduce these elements in the following order:

Proper names of people
(both first and last name) .... Weeks 5–6

Proper names of cities .... Weeks 7–8

Proper names of states .... Weeks 9–10

Once an element is introduced, continue to include it in the copywork on occasion.

If you cannot find sentences that contain these elements, alternate choosing copywork sentences from the student's books and making up your own copywork sentences with these elements included; this will help the student to practice proper form.

Year One, Weeks 11–19

Copywork sentences grow slightly longer (around six to ten words); names of days and months are introduced, as well as pronouns. Narration exercises consist of slightly longer paragraphs, continuing to develop the student's memory and retention. The student continues to use his own sentences for copywork.

Week 11 spells out this development; Weeks 12 through 19 are modeled on the pattern of Week 11.

WEEK 11

DAY ONE: Copywork

Copy out one of the following sentences on first-grade lined paper, in neat print handwriting, for the student to copy. Choose whichever length is appropriate to the student's handwriting ability.

Explain to the student that these sentences are from *The Trumpet of the Swan*, by E. B. White. The book is about a young trumpeter swan named Louis who is born without a voice. A young boy named Sam Beaver becomes his friend. Since he can't speak, Louis learns how to write on a slate—and also how to play a real trumpet.

Louis is a musician.

He came here from Montana with Sam Beaver.

DAY TWO: Narration Exercise

Tell the student that the following scene takes place near the beginning of the book. Louis and his brothers and sisters have just hatched out of their eggs, and their parents are taking them for their very first swim. Sam Beaver is sitting quietly by the pond, watching them. Explain that a "cob" is a male swan, and that "cygnet" is the name for a baby swan.

> Like all fathers, the cob wanted to show off his children to somebody. So he led the cygnets to where Sam was. They all stepped out of the water and stood in front of the boy—all but the mother swan. She stayed behind.
>
> "Ko-hoh!" said the cob.

"Hello!" said Sam, who hadn't expected anything like this and hardly dared breathe.

The first cygnet looked at Sam and said, "Beep." The second cygnet looked at Sam and said, "Beep." The third cygnet greeted Sam the same way. So did the fourth. The fifth cygnet was different. He opened his mouth but didn't say a thing. He made an effort to say beep, but no sound came. So instead, he stuck his little neck out, took hold of one of Sam's shoelaces, and gave it a pull. He tugged the lace for a moment. It came untied. Then he let it go. It was like a greeting. Sam grinned.

The cob now looked worried. He ran his long white neck between the cygnets and the boy and guided the babies back to the water and to their mother.

"Follow me!" said the cob. And he led them off, full of grace and bursting with pride.

—From *The Trumpet of the Swan*
by E. B. White

Ask the following questions:

Instructor: Which parent took the cygnets to see Sam Beaver—their mother or their father?
Student: Their father took them.

Instructor: What is a male swan called?
Student: A male swan is called a cob.

Instructor: What did most of the cygnets say to Sam?
Student: They said "Beep."

Instructor: Why was the fifth cygnet different?
Student: He couldn't say anything.

Instructor: What did he do instead?
Student: He pulled on Sam's shoelace.

Instructor: Where did the cob take the babies after they met Sam?
Student: *He took them back to the water OR back to their mother.*

Ask, "What is one thing you remember about the passage?" Write the student's answer down on first-grade lined paper as he watches.

Day Three: Copywork
Copy out one of the following sentences on first-grade lined paper, in neat print handwriting, for the student to copy. Choose whichever length is appropriate to the student's handwriting ability.

Explain to the student that, in the story, Louis decides to leave his home and explore other places.

Louis had no trouble finding Philadelphia.

They flew south across Maryland and Virginia.

Day Four: Narration Exercise and Copywork
In this scene, Louis's father has realized that his young son can't speak. He decides to go and find Louis a trumpet in the nearby city of Billings, Montana.

Toward the end of the afternoon, the cob looked ahead and in the distance saw the churches and factories and shops and homes of Billings. He decided to act quickly and boldly. He circled the city once, looking for a music store. Suddenly he spied one. It had a very big, wide window, solid glass. The cob flew lower and circled so that he could get a better look. He gazed into the store. He saw a drum painted gold. He saw a fancy guitar with an electric cord. He saw a small piano. He saw banjos, horns, violins, mandolins, cymbals, saxophones, marimbaphones, cellos, and many other instruments. Then he saw what he wanted: he saw a brass trumpet hanging by a red cord.

"Now is my time to act!" he said to himself. "Now is my

moment for risking everything on one bold move, however shocking it may be to my sensibilities, however offensive it may be to the laws that govern the lives of men. Here I go! May good luck go with me!"

With that, the old cob set his wings for a dive. He aimed straight at the big window. He held his neck stiff and straight, waiting for the crash. He dove swiftly and hit the window going full speed. The glass broke. The noise was terrific. The whole store shook. Musical instruments fell to the floor. Glass flew everywhere. A salesgirl fainted. The cob felt a twinge of pain as a jagged piece of broken glass cut into his shoulder, but he grabbed the trumpet in his beak, turned sharply in the air, flew back through the hole in the window, and began climbing fast over the roofs of Billings. A few drops of blood fell to the ground below. His shoulder hurt. But he had succeeded in getting what he had come for. Held firmly in his bill, its red cord dangling, was a beautiful brass trumpet.

—From *The Trumpet of the Swan*
by E. B. White

Ask the following questions:

Instructor: What was the cob looking for, as he circled the city?
Student: He was looking for a music store.

Instructor: Can you name three things that the cob saw inside the store?
Student: He saw a drum, a guitar, a piano, banjos, horns, violins, mandolins, cymbals, saxophones, marimbaphones, and cellos.

Instructor: How did the cob get into the store?
Student: He broke through the window.

Instructor: Did he hurt himself? Where?
Student: Yes, he hurt his shoulder.

Instructor: When he flew away, what was he holding in his bill?

Student: *He was holding a beautiful brass trumpet.*

Ask, "What is one thing you remember about the passage?" Write the student's answer down on first-grade lined paper as he watches.

Place this written answer in front of the student. Ask him to copy the sentence in pencil on the line below the model. If the sentence is too long for comfort, he can copy only the first eight to ten words.

WEEKS 12–19

Follow the same weekly pattern as above:

Day One: Copywork

Day Two: Narration Exercise

Day Three: Copywork

Day Four: Narration Exercise and Copywork

Choose sentences of six to ten words and narrations of approximately three slightly longer paragraphs from the student's history, science, and literature books.

Over these eight weeks, look for copywork sentences that contain the proper names of days of the week and months of the year, the pronoun "I" (occurring in the middle of the sentence), and other subject and object pronouns.

Introduce these elements in the following order:

Names of days of the week and holidays.......... Weeks 12–13

Names of months of the year .... Weeks 14–16

The pronoun "I" (occurring in the middle of a sentence) .... Week 17

Other subject and object pronouns (you, he, him, she, her, it, we, us, they, them).............. Weeks 18–19

If you cannot find sentences that contain these elements, alternate choosing copywork sentences from the student's books and making up your own copywork sentences with these elements included; this will help the student to practice proper form.

Year One, Weeks 20–27

Copywork sentences lengthen to eight to eleven words and introduce abbreviations, titles of respect, the seasons, and proper usage. Narrations lengthen to approximately three long or four shorter paragraphs. The student continues to use his own narration sentences for copywork.

Week 20 spells out these developments; Weeks 21 through 27 are modeled on the Week 20 pattern.

WEEK 20

Day One: Copywork

Copy out one of the following sentences on first-grade lined paper, in neat print handwriting, for the student to copy. Choose whichever length is appropriate to the student's handwriting ability.

A. A. Milne wrote stories about Piglet and Pooh.

The writer A. A. Milne really did have a son named Christopher Robin.

Ask the student to look carefully at the sentences. While she is examining the sentences, explain that these sentences are about the author of the Winnie-the-Pooh stories. His full name was Alan Alexander Milne. We can abbreviate, or shorten, a proper name by writing the first letter of the name and putting a period after it. This kind of abbreviation is called an initial. A. A. are the initials for Alan Alexander.

Day Two: Narration Exercise

Tell the student the following passage is from *A Child's Geography of the World*, by V. M. Hillyer. He wrote this book over fifty years ago.

> All around the outside of the world—as you probably know—is an ocean of air that covers everything on the world as the ocean of water covers everything in the sea. What you probably don't know is that this ocean of air is wrapped only round the world—it does not fill the sky. Men and animals live in this ocean of air as fish live in the ocean of water, and

if a huge giant picked you out of the air you would die just as quickly as a fish does when taken out of the sea. The air is thick near the ground but gets thinner and thinner the higher up you go off the ground. That's why airplanes can go up but a few miles high—there is not enough air to hold up the plane, for the plane must have air to rest on and for its propeller to push against, just as a boat in the water must have water to rest on and water for its propeller to push against. Or if it's a jet plane, it must have air to feed its jet motors. An airplane could not rise beyond the ocean of air and sail off into the sky where there is no air any more than a steamship on the sea could rise out of the water and sail off up into the air.

There is only one thing that men can send up high enough to travel above the ocean of air. This is a rocket, which doesn't depend on air for its motor or to hold it up.....

Some mountains are so high that their tops almost stick out of the ocean of air; at least, there is so little air covering their tops that people can't go all the way to the top unless they take along canned air to breathe.

You can't see air—you may think you can, but what you see is smoke or clouds, not air. When air is moving, we call it wind. Then you can feel it when it blows your hat off, you can hear it when it bangs the shutters and whistles round the house; but no one has ever seen air itself.

—From *A Child's Geography of the World*
by V. M. Hillyer

Ask the following questions. Remind the student to answer you in complete sentences. If she answers in a fragment, turn the fragment into a complete sentence, say it to her, and then ask her to repeat this sentence back to you. If she cannot answer a question, read her the part of the passage that contains the answer, and then ask the question again.

Instructor: What kind of ocean wraps all the way around the world?
Student: *An ocean of air covers the world.*

Instructor: The air is thick near the ground. What happens as it gets higher and higher?

Student: *The air gets thinner and thinner.*

Instructor: What does an airplane need for its propeller to push against?

Student: *It must have air.*

Instructor: Why can't an airplane fly up above the "ocean of air"?

Student: *The air is too thin.*

Instructor: What is the one thing that people can send up above the ocean of air?

Student: *People can send up a rocket.*

Instructor: On very high mountains, what is the air like at the top?

Student: *The air is so thin that people can't breathe.*

Instructor: What do we call air that is moving?

Student: *We call it wind.*

Instructor: Can you see the air?

Student: *No; you can only see smoke or clouds.*

Ask, "What is one thing you remember about the passage?" Write the student's answer down on first-grade lined paper as she watches.

DAY THREE: Copywork

Copy out one of the following sentences on first-grade lined paper, in neat print handwriting, for the student to copy. Choose whichever length is appropriate to the student's handwriting ability.

V. M. Hillyer wrote a book about geography for children.

V. M. Hillyer thought that children should also

study maps, collect stamps, and make scrapbooks
about the world.

Explain to the student that these sentences are about the author of *A Child's Geography of the World*. Ask the student to point to the initials in Mr. Hillyer's name. Remind her that an initial is the first letter of a person's name, followed by a period. Initials are capital letters, because names begin with capital letters.

DAY FOUR: Narration Exercise and Copywork
Read the following passage from *A Child's Geography of the World* out loud to the student.

> The outside of the world is a crust of rock like the skin of a baked potato over the hot inside. Some of the crust that you go through first is in layers, like layers in a jelly-cake, one layer after another, only these rock layers look as if they were made of sand and shells, or coal or little stones, and that's what they *are* made of.....
>
> Between some of the layers of the rock there is coal like jelly in a jelly-cake and in other places there are gold and silver and diamonds and rubies, and in some of the rock there are pools of oil. That's why men dig wells down through these layers of rock to get oil, and that's why men dig mines to get coal and gold.
>
> And still farther down the rock is not layers—it is just solid rock; and still farther down it gets hotter and hotter where the world has not cooled off even yet, until the rock is no longer solid, but melted.
>
> When ever you see a chimney you know there is a furnace beneath it, and when smoke and fire come out of its top you know there is a fire in the furnace. Well, there are many places in the world where fire and smoke come out of the ground as if through a chimney from a fiery furnace. These places are called volcanoes.

—from *A Child's Geography of the World*
by V. M. Hillyer

Ask the following questions. Remind the student to answer you in complete sentences. If she answers in a fragment, turn the fragment into a complete sentence, say it to her, and then ask her to repeat this sentence back to you. If she cannot answer a question, read her the part of the passage that contains the answer, and then ask the question again.

Instructor: What is the crust on the outside of the world made of?
Student: *The crust is made of rock.*

Instructor: Can you name two of the four common things that the rock layers are made out of?
Student: *The layers are made out of sand, shells, coal, and little stones.*

Instructor: Can you name two of the four valuable things that sometimes lie between the layers?
Student: *Gold, silver, diamonds, and rubies lie between the layers.*

Instructor: What kinds of pools lie in some of the rock?
Student: *Pools of oil lie in some of the rock.*

Instructor: What do people dig to get the oil out?
Student: *They dig wells.*

Instructor: What do people dig to get the coal and gold out?
Student: *They dig mines.*

Instructor: What is the rock like far, far down at the center of the earth?
Student: *It is melted because it is so hot.*

Instructor: What do we call the places where fire and smoke come out of the ground?
Student: *We call them volcanoes.*

Ask "What is one thing you remember about the passage?" Write the student's answer down on first-grade lined paper as she watches. This answer can be the same as one of the answers above.

Place this written answer in front of the student. Ask her to copy one of the sentences in pencil below the model.

WEEKS 21–27

Follow the same pattern as above:

DAY ONE: Copywork

DAY TWO: Narration Exercise

DAY THREE: Copywork

DAY FOUR: Narration Exercise and Copywork

Choose sentences of eight to eleven words (or slightly longer, if the student is writing with ease) and narrations of three long or four briefer paragraphs from the student's history, science, and literature books. Over these eight weeks, look for copywork sentences that contain the following elements, in order:

Initials (as an abbreviation for a proper name) . Week 21
The seasons (summer, winter, spring, fall) .... Weeks 22–23
Abbreviations for months of the year.............. Week 24
Proper usage of the verbs "sit" and "set" .... Week 25
The titles Mr., Mrs., Dr., Miss, Ms. .... Weeks 26–27

If you cannot find sentences that contain these elements, alternate choosing copywork sentences from the student's books and making up your own copywork sentences with these elements included; this will help the student to practice proper form.

Year One, Weeks 28–35

Copywork sentences are now ten to twelve words (or slightly longer, if the student is writing with ease) and introduce proper poetic form, dates, and a variety of ending punctuation marks. Narrations lengthen to four or five brief paragraphs. The student should be able to copy out an entire sentence of his own narration.

Week 28 spells out these developments; Weeks 29 through 35 are modeled on the Week 28 pattern.

WEEK 28

DAY ONE: Copywork

Copy out one of the following sentences on first-grade lined paper, in neat print handwriting, for the student to copy. Choose whichever length is appropriate to the student's handwriting ability.

Explain to the student that these sentences are from *Little House on the Prairie*, another book written by Laura Ingalls Wilder. After the events in *Little House in the Big Woods*, which we read from back in Week 1, the Ingalls family moved away from their little Wisconsin house, further west into unsettled land. There were no other houses or towns on the prairies (huge, wide open fields) where they decided to settle down, so Laura's father and another settler, Mr. Scott, had to dig a well so that the family could have clean drinking water.

> In the morning Mr. Scott slid down the rope and dug.

> The buckets came up full of mud, and Pa and Mr. Scott worked every day in deeper mud.

> > —From *Little House on the Prairie*
> > by Laura Ingalls Wilder

DAY TWO: Narration Exercise

Today's narration exercise describes the end of the well-digging project. For days, Pa and Mr. Scott have been taking turns going down into the hole, digging up the dirt at the bottom, and sending it back up to the surface in a bucket. They have to dig until the hole is deep enough to reach "ground water"—the water that collects in pools under the earth's surface.

You may need to explain that "bailing" is taking out bucketfuls of water and dumping them somewhere else.

> There began to be a little water in the well, but it was not enough. The buckets came up full of mud, and Pa and Mr. Scott worked every day in deeper mud. In the mornings when the candle went down, it lighted oozing-wet walls, and candlelight sparkled in rings over the water when the bucket struck bottom.
>
> Pa stood knee deep in water and bailed out bucketfuls before he could begin digging in the mud.
>
> One day when he was digging, a loud shout came echoing up. Ma ran out of the house and Laura ran to the well. "Pull, Scott! Pull!" Pa yelled. A swishing, gurgling sound echoed down there. Mr. Scott turned the windlass as fast as he could, and Pa came up climbing hand over hand up the rope.
>
> "I'm blamed if that's not quicksand!" Pa gasped, as he stepped onto the ground, muddy and dripping. "I was pushing down hard on the spade, when all of a sudden it went down, the whole length of the handle. And water came pouring up all around me."

—From *Little House on the Prairie*
by Laura Ingalls Wilder

Ask the following questions:

Instructor: What did Pa and Mr. Scott use for light while they were digging in the hole?
Student: They had to use a candle.

Instructor: What did Pa have to do before he could start digging?
Student: He had to bail out water.

Instructor: How did Pa get up out of the well?
Student: He climbed up the rope.

Instructor: What did Pa find in the bottom of the well?
Student: There was quicksand in the bottom of the well.

Instructor: What happened when Pa pushed down hard on his spade?
Student: Water came pouring up.

Ask, "What is one thing you remember about the passage?" Remember to help the student answer in a complete sentence. Write the student's answer down on first-grade lined paper as he watches.

DAY THREE: Copywork Exercise

Copy out one of the following sets of sentences on first-grade lined paper, in neat print handwriting, for the student to copy. Choose whichever length is appropriate to the student's handwriting ability.

Explain that these sentences come from the next book about the Ingalls family, *On the Banks of Plum Creek*. Pa, Ma, Laura, and Laura's sisters have moved again. Now they are living in Minnesota, trying to make a living by farming. But their corn, barley, and garden vegetables are all eaten by swarms of grasshoppers who sweep down over their farm.

Set One:

Grasshoppers beat down from the sky and swarmed thick over the ground.

Set Two:

Millions and millions of grasshoppers were eating now. You could hear the millions of jaws biting and chewing.

—From *On the Banks of Plum Creek*
by Laura Ingalls Wilder

DAY FOUR: Narration Exercise and Copywork

Explain to the student that, when the grasshoppers first appeared, Laura didn't realize that she was looking at a swarm of insects. There were so many of them that she thought they were a stormcloud! (In the story, Jack is the family's dog.)

> A cloud was over the sun. It was not like any cloud they had ever seen before. It was a cloud of something like snowflakes, but they were larger than snowflakes, and thin and glittering. Light shone through each flickering particle.
>
> There was no wind. The grasses were still and the hot air did not stir, but the edge of the cloud came on across the sky faster than wind. The hair stood up on Jack's neck. All at once he made a frightful sound up at that cloud, a growl and a whine.
>
> Plunk! Something hit Laura's head and fell to the ground. She looked down and saw the largest grasshopper she had ever seen. Then huge brown grasshoppers were hitting the ground all around her, hitting her head and her face and her arms. They came thudding down like hail.
>
> The cloud was hailing grasshoppers. The cloud *was* grasshoppers. Their bodies hid the sun and made darkness. Their thin, large wings gleamed and glittered. The rasping whirring of their wings filled the whole air and they hit the ground and the house with the noise of a hailstorm.
>
> Laura tried to beat them off. Their claws clung to her skin and her dress. They looked at her with bulging eyes, turning their heads this way and that. Mary ran screaming into the house. Grasshoppers covered the ground, there was not one bare bit to step on. Laura had to step on grasshoppers and they smashed squirming and slimy under her feet.

—From *On the Banks of Plum Creek*
by Laura Ingalls Wilder

Ask the following questions:

> **Instructor:** What did Laura think that the grasshopper cloud looked like?
> *Student: It looked like a cloud of snowflakes.*

> **Instructor:** Was the wind blowing?
> *Student: No, there was no wind.*

> **Instructor:** What did Jack the dog do when he saw the cloud?
> *Student: He growled and hair stood up on his neck.*

> **Instructor:** What did the grasshopper cloud do to the sun?
> *Student: It hid the sun.*

> **Instructor:** What kind of eyes did the grasshoppers have?
> *Student: They had bulging eyes.*

> **Instructor:** What did Mary do?
> *Student: She ran into the house screaming.*

> **Instructor:** What happened when Laura stepped on the ground?
> *Student: She stepped on grasshoppers and they smashed under her feet.*

Ask, "What is one thing you remember about the passage?" Write the student's answer down on first-grade lined paper as he watches.

Place this written answer in front of the student. Ask him to copy the sentence in pencil on the line below the model. He should be able to copy the entire sentence.

WEEKS 29–35

Follow the same pattern as above.

DAY ONE: Copywork

DAY TWO: Narration Exercise

DAY THREE: Copywork

DAY FOUR: Narration Exercise and Copywork

Choose sentences of ten to twelve words (or slightly longer, if the student is writing with ease) and narrations of approximately four or five brief paragraphs from the student's history, science, and literature books. Over these seven weeks, look for copywork sentences that contain the following elements, in order:

Review proper names and titles of respect .... Week 29
Lines from poems (reproducing original capitalization and punctuation) .... Weeks 30–31
Commands and statements (ending with periods) .... Week 32
Questions (ending with question marks) .... Week 33
Exclamations (ending with exclamation points) . Weeks 34–35

If you cannot find sentences that contain these elements, alternate choosing copywork sentences from the student's books and making up your own copywork sentences with these elements included; this will help the student to practice proper form.

Year One Mastery Evaluation, Week 36

This week's assignments are designed to evaluate the student's mastery of the Year One skills. Before moving to Year Two, the student should be able to copy a ten-word sentence without error, accurately answer questions about a passage approximately four to five paragraphs in length, and answer the question "What is one thing you remember about the passage?" with a complete sentence. Feel free to give some help, but if the student is frustrated by any of these assignments, spend some additional time working on copywork or narration before moving on to Year Two.

DAY ONE: Copywork

Copy out the following sentences on first-grade lined paper, in neat print handwriting. Ask the student to copy them out in her own handwriting below your model. Remind the student that her copy should look exactly like the model, but do not give other specific suggestions.

> The rain is falling all around,
> It falls on field and tree,
> It rains on the umbrellas here,
> And on the ships at sea.

—From *A Child's Garden of Verses*
by Robert Louis Stevenson

If the student misspells more than one word and does not reproduce the punctuation and capitalization properly, spend a few more weeks on copywork before moving on to Year Two.

DAY TWO: Narration Exercise

Tell the student that this excerpt is from the beginning of *The Wonderful Wizard of Oz*, by L. Frank Baum. In this story, a little girl named Dorothy is picked up by a cyclone (a tornado) and taken to a magical country called Oz. Toto is Dorothy's little dog.

The student may need to be prompted for the answer to one of the questions that follow, but if she doesn't know the answers to two or three of the questions, she should practice listening on more passages of this length before going on to Year Two.

You may need to remind the student to answer in complete sentences, but you should not have to form the complete sentences for her. If so, she needs additional practice before going on to Year Two.

> From the far north they heard a low wail of the wind, and Uncle Henry and Dorothy could see where the long grass bowed in waves before the coming storm. There now came a sharp whistling in the air from the south, and as they turned their eyes that way they saw ripples in the grass coming from that direction also.
>
> Suddenly Uncle Henry stood up.
>
> "There's a cyclone coming, Em," he called to his wife. "I'll go look after the stock." Then he ran toward the sheds where the cows and horses were kept.
>
> Aunt Em dropped her work and came to the door. One glance told her of the danger close at hand.
>
> "Quick, Dorothy!" she screamed. "Run for the cellar!"
>
> Toto jumped out of Dorothy's arms and hid under the bed, and the girl started to get him. Aunt Em, badly frightened, threw open the trap door in the floor and climbed down the ladder into the small, dark hole. Dorothy caught Toto at last and started to follow her aunt. When she was halfway across the room there came a great shriek from the wind, and the house shook so hard that she lost her footing and sat down suddenly upon the floor.
>
> Then a strange thing happened.
>
> The house whirled around two or three times and rose slowly through the air. Dorothy felt as if she were going up in a balloon.
>
> The north and south winds met where the house stood, and made it the exact center of the cyclone. In the middle of a cyclone the air is generally still, but the great pressure of the wind on every side of the house raised it up higher and higher, until it was at the very top of the cyclone; and there it remained and was carried miles and miles away as easily as you could carry a feather.

—From *The Wonderful Wizard of Oz*
by L. Frank Baum

Ask the following questions:

Instructor: What are the names of Dorothy's uncle and aunt?
Student: *They are named Uncle Henry and Aunt Em.*

Instructor: Dorothy and Uncle Henry saw and heard three things that warned them of the coming cyclone. Can you remember one of them?
Student: *They heard the wind wail* **OR** *They saw ripples in the grass* **OR** *They heard whistling in the air.*

Instructor: Where did Uncle Henry go, after he warned Aunt Em about the cyclone?
Student: *He ran to the sheds where the cows and horses were.*

Instructor: Where did Toto go?
Student: *Toto hid under the bed.*

Instructor: Where did Aunt Em go?
Student: *She went through the trap door in the floor.*

Instructor: What happened to Dorothy and the house?
Student: *They were carried up into the cyclone.*

Ask, "What is one thing you remember about the passage?" Remember to help the student answer in a complete sentence. Write the student's answer down on first-grade lined paper as she watches.

DAY THREE: Copywork

Copy out the following sentences on first-grade lined paper, in neat print handwriting, for the student to copy. Remind the student that the copied sentences should look exactly like the original, but do not give any other specific reminders.

L. Frank Baum wrote stories about a little girl who lived in Kansas. Her name was Dorothy, and she went to the land of Oz.

If the student misspells more than one word and does not reproduce the punctuation and capitalization properly, spend a few more weeks on copywork before moving on to Year Two.

DAY FOUR: Narration Exercise and Copywork

Tell the student that, after Dorothy landed in the land of Oz, she found herself in the land of the Munchkins, peaceful farmers who wore blue. She left the Munchkins to go to the city of Oz, because she thought that the wizard who lived there might be able to help her get back to Kansas.

The student may need to be prompted for the answer to one of the questions that follow, but if she doesn't know the answers to two or three of the questions, she should practice listening on more passages of this length before going on to Year Two.

You may need to remind the student to answer in complete sentences, but you should not have to form the complete sentences for her. If so, she needs additional practice before going on to Year Two.

> She bade her friends good-bye, and again started along the road of yellow brick. When she had gone several miles she thought she would stop to rest, and so climbed to the top of the fence beside the road and sat down. There was a great cornfield beyond the fence, and not far away she saw a Scarecrow, placed high on a pole to keep the birds from the ripe corn.
>
> Dorothy leaned her chin upon her hand and gazed thoughtfully at the Scarecrow. Its head was a small sack stuffed with straw, with eyes, nose, and mouth painted on it to represent a face.
>
> An old, pointed blue hat, that had belonged to some Munchkin, was perched on his head, and the rest of the figure was a blue suit of clothes, worn and faded, which had also been stuffed with straw. On the feet were some old boots with blue

tops, such as every man wore in this country, and the figure was raised above the stalks of corn by means of the pole stuck up its back.

While Dorothy was looking earnestly into the queer, painted face of the Scarecrow, she was surprised to see one of the eyes slowly wink at her. She thought she must have been mistaken at first, for none of the scarecrows in Kansas ever wink; but presently the figure nodded its head to her in a friendly way. Then she climbed down from the fence and walked up to it, while Toto ran around the pole and barked.

"Good day," said the Scarecrow, in a rather husky voice.

"Did you speak?" asked the girl, in wonder.

"Certainly," answered the Scarecrow. "How do you do?"

"I'm pretty well, thank you," replied Dorothy politely. "How do you do?"

"I'm not feeling well," said the Scarecrow, with a smile, "for it is very tedious being perched up here night and day to scare away crows."

—From *The Wonderful Wizard of Oz*
by L. Frank Baum

Ask the following questions:

Instructor: What kind of road did Dorothy follow?
Student: She followed a road of yellow brick.

Instructor: What did she see when she sat on the fence beside the road?
Student: She saw a Scarecrow.

Instructor: Why was the Scarecrow in the field?
Student: He was there to scare the crows away from the crops.

Instructor: What color was the Scarecrow wearing?
Student: He was wearing blue.

Instructor: How did Dorothy know that the Scarecrow was alive?
Student: He winked at her.

Instructor: Was the Scarecrow content to be on his pole?
Student: No; he was bored with scaring crows.

Ask, "What is one thing you remember about the passage?" Remember to help the student answer in a complete sentence. Write the student's answer down on first-grade lined paper as she watches.

Place this written answer in front of the student. Ask her to copy the sentence in pencil on the line below the model.

Year Two
Second Grade (or Level Two, for Older Writers)

In Year Two, the student will continue working on the two most basic skills of writing (taking thoughts and putting them into words, and then taking words and putting them down on paper) separately, until both skills are fully mastered.

The first skill (taking thoughts and putting them into words) is still practiced through narration. During Year One, the student learned to put thoughts into complete sentences, ready to be set down on paper. In Year Two, the student will exercise this skill on longer passages. She will also develop the skill of finding the central thought of a reading selection. You will still prepare her for her narration exercise by asking specific questions about the passage, but she will learn to answer the more general question "What is this passage about?" This question (as opposed to "What is one thing your remember about this passage?") requires the student to identify the most important element of the passage. This ability is vital for writing; until the student can pick out the central idea of a passage, she will be unable to clarify, in her own original writing, exactly *what* any given paragraph (or composition) is about. Her writing will remain a mass of jumbled ideas without order.

In Year One, the student practiced the second skill (taking words and putting them down on paper) through copywork. Now that her mind is well stocked with images of written language, she will begin to do dictation instead; this will require her to picture a written sentence in her head before putting it down on paper, and will force her to access her memory of proper grammar, punctuation, and capitalization as she writes. Too often, students never make the connection with their language knowledge as they write; they are too busy struggling with the ideas. Dictation removes the difficulty of coming up with ideas, and allows the beginning writer to develop the habit of connecting his grammar and style knowledge with his written work.

The lessons that follow spell out an entire week's assignments whenever the student progresses from one step to the next. If you wish, you can then follow the pattern of this model work, but choose your own copywork and narration assignments. Alternatively, you can use the Year Two workbook; this provides a full sequence of copywork and narration assignments that introduce the student sequentially to the necessary grammatical elements.

Year Two, Weeks 1–10

The student begins dictation by first copying a sentence of ten to twelve words, and then taking the sentence from dictation on another day. Narration passages are around four paragraphs long, or 15 to 17 lines (these are only general guidelines, since shorter passages can be denser and more difficult to remember than passages containing many short lines of dialogue). After answering comprehension questions, the student will learn to identify the most important element of the passage. Narration sentences will also be used for dictation, just as narration sentences were used for copywork in Year One.

The pattern established in Week 1 will be followed in Weeks 2 through 10.

WEEK 1

DAY ONE: Narration Exercise

After reading this passage to the student, you will help him identify the three central actions that form the "skeleton" of the plot. This begins to train the student to summarize narrative passages.

Read aloud:

> The Owl always takes her sleep during the day. Then after sundown, when the rosy light fades from the sky and the shadows rise slowly through the wood, out she comes ruffling and blinking from the old hollow tree. Now her weird "hoo-hoo-hoo-oo-oo" echoes through the quiet wood, and she begins her hunt for the bugs and beetles, frogs and mice she likes so well to eat.
>
> Now there was a certain old Owl who had become very cross and hard to please as she grew older, especially if anything disturbed her daily slumbers. One warm summer afternoon as she dozed away in her den in the old oak tree, a Grasshopper nearby began a joyous but very raspy song. Out popped the old Owl's head from the opening in the tree that served her both for door and for window.
>
> "Get away from here, sir," she said to the Grasshopper. "Have you no manners? You should at least respect my age and

leave me to sleep in quiet!"

But the Grasshopper answered saucily that he had as much right to his place in the sun as the Owl had to her place in the old oak. Then he struck up a louder and still more rasping tune.

The wise old Owl knew quite well that it would do no good to argue with the Grasshopper, nor with anybody else for that matter. Besides, her eyes were not sharp enough by day to permit her to punish the Grasshopper as he deserved. So she laid aside all hard words and spoke very kindly to him.

"Well sir," she said, "if I must stay awake, I am going to settle right down to enjoy your singing. Now that I think of it, I have a wonderful wine here, sent me from Olympus, of which I am told Apollo drinks before he sings to the high gods. Please come up and taste this delicious drink with me. I know it will make you sing like Apollo himself."

The foolish Grasshopper was taken in by the Owl's flattering words. Up he jumped to the Owl's den, but as soon as he was near enough so the old Owl could see him clearly, she pounced upon him and ate him up.

Moral: Just because someone flatters you, it doesn't mean that they truly admire you.

—"The Owl and the Grasshopper"
by Aesop

Ask the following questions to test the student's listening ability. Remind the student to answer in complete sentences; if he answers in a fragment, put the answer in the form of a sentence and then require the student to repeat it back to you.

Instructor: When does the Owl sleep?
Student: She sleeps during the day.

Instructor: What did the Grasshopper do to annoy the owl?
Student: He began a very noisy, raspy song.

Instructor: When the Owl told the Grasshopper to be quiet, what did the Grasshopper do?
Student: He began to sing more loudly.

Instructor: Why did the Owl decide not to punish the Grasshopper at once?
Student: She couldn't see well enough during the day to catch him.

Instructor: What did the Owl offer to the Grasshopper?
Student: She offered him the wine of Apollo.

Instructor: What happened to the Grasshopper when he flew up to drink the wine?
Student: The Owl ate him.

Your goal now is to teach the student to summarize the basic narrative thread in the passage—the "bones" of the selection—in not more than two sentences. In order to do this, say to the student:

Instructor: What problem did the Owl have?
Student: The Grasshopper was keeping the Owl awake.

Instructor: How did the Owl get rid of the Grasshopper?
Student: She invited the Grasshopper to come drink wine with her, and then she ate him.

NOTE: If the student just gives you one part of this answer, encourage him to give a two-part answer by saying:

Instructor: What did the Owl invite the Grasshopper to do?
Student: She invited him to drink wine.

Instructor: Then what did she do?
Student: She ate him.

Now ask the student, "Can you tell me in one or two sentences what happened in this story?" The student's answer should resemble one of the following (three BRIEF sentences are also acceptable):

"The Grasshopper was making so much noise that the Owl couldn't sleep. He wouldn't be quiet, so she invited him to have wine, and then she ate him."

"The Grasshopper wouldn't stop singing when the Owl asked him to. So she flattered him, and then she ate him up."

"The Owl couldn't sleep because the Grasshopper was singing. So she told him that he was a wonderful singer and offered him wine. When he flew up to drink it, she ate him."

Write down the student's narration as he watches.

As you can see, students cannot learn to summarize effectively until they are guided into recognizing the important elements of stories through careful questioning. Your questioning and conversation will help the student learn to discard unimportant details and keep only the central parts of the narrative.

DAY TWO: Copywork

The following sentence is another way to phrase the moral of "The Owl and the Grasshopper." Point out that the article before "enemy" is "an" rather than "a" because "enemy" begins with a vowel rather than a consonant.

Copy this sentence out on second-grade lined paper for the student to look at as he writes. Remember to watch him write, and correct him at once if he begins to make errors in spelling or format.

> Do not let flattery throw you off your guard
> against an enemy.

DAY THREE: The First Dictation Exercise

Tips for Teaching

Now that the student has experience in writing properly while looking at a sentence, he'll learn how to *visualize* a properly written sentence in his head before he puts it down on paper.

For this reason, the first dictation exercise is the sentence which the student copied the day before. Although you won't show the sentence to the student before dictating it, he should have some memory of it.

Just as with beginning copywork, allow the student to write in pencil. Watch him as he writes; if he begins to make a mistake in form or spelling, stop him and tell him the correct answer. Never let him write incorrectly; the point of the exercise is to reinforce *correct* mental pictures of written language.

If the student asks you how to spell a word, tell him; this is not a spelling exercise.

This dictation sentence does not contain any punctuation challenges. If necessary, remind the student that this is a command, and that commands are sentences which begin with capital letters and end with periods or exclamation points. Since this is not an urgent command, it ends with a period.

Tell the student that you will read the following sentence slowly, twice. He should pay close attention so that he can remember the sentence and write it down.

After you have repeated the sentence the second time, encourage the student to repeat it back to you. After he repeats it, tell him to write it down.

If the student forgets the last part of the sentence, you can read it to him again. However, first tell him to read out loud what he's already written, and see whether he can then say the rest of the sentence himself.

If you do then have to repeat the last part of the sentence out loud, ask the student to repeat the forgotten words back to you before he writes. You are helping the student develop the skill of active listening as he writes, which will be necessary when he does his own original work later.

Do not let flattery throw you off your guard against an enemy.

Day Four: Narration Exercise and Dictation

Today's exercise will combine narration and dictation. Tell the student that you will read the following passage to him, ask him a few questions about it, and then help him to summarize it in two or three sentences. After you write these sentences down (while the student watches), you will dictate one or two of them back to him.

The Fox one day thought of a plan to amuse himself at the

expense of the Stork, at whose odd appearance he was always laughing.

"You must come and dine with me today," he said to the Stork, smiling to himself at the trick he was going to play. The Stork gladly accepted the invitation and arrived in good time and with a very good appetite.

For dinner the Fox served soup. But it was set out in a very shallow dish, and all the Stork could do was to wet the very tip of his bill. Not a drop of soup could he get. But the Fox lapped it up easily, and, to increase the disappointment of the Stork, made a great show of enjoyment.

The hungry Stork was much displeased at the trick, but he was a calm, even-tempered fellow and saw no good in flying into a rage. Instead, not long afterward, he invited the Fox to dine with him in turn.

The Fox arrived promptly at the time that had been set, and the Stork served a fish dinner that had a very appetizing smell. But it was served in a tall jar with a very narrow neck. The Stork could easily get at the food with his long bill, but all the Fox could do was to lick the outside of the jar, and sniff at the delicious odor. And when the Fox lost his temper, the Stork said calmly, "Do not play tricks on your neighbors unless you can stand the same treatment yourself."

—"The Fox and the Stork"
by Aesop

Ask the following questions to test the student's listening ability. Remind the student to answer in complete sentences; if he answers in a fragment, put the answer in the form of a sentence and then require the student to repeat it back to you.

Instructor: Why did the Fox laugh at the Stork?
Student: *He laughed at the Stork's odd appearance.*

Instructor: What did the Fox serve the Stork for dinner?
Student: *He served soup.*

Instructor: Why did the Stork have trouble eating the soup?
Student: He could not get his bill down into the shallow dish.

Instructor: What did the Stork serve the Fox in return?
Student: He served the Fox fish.

Instructor: Why couldn't the Fox eat the fish?
Student: It was in a tall jar with a narrow opening.

Instructor: What is the moral of this fable?
Student: If you play tricks on people, you shouldn't be upset when they play tricks on you **OR** *Don't play tricks on people unless you don't mind having tricks played on you* **OR** *an equivalent answer.*

You will now continue to teach the student to summarize the basic narrative thread in the passage. In order to do this, say to the student:

Instructor: What did the Fox do to the Stork?
Student: He served the Stork dinner in a dish too shallow for the Stork to eat out of.

Instructor: What did the Stork do to the Fox in return?
Student: He served the Fox dinner in a jar with a very narrow top.

Instructor: What did the Stork say to the Fox at the end of the story?
Student: Don't play tricks on people if you don't want tricks played on you.

Now ask the student, "Can you tell me in two sentences what happened in this story?" The student's answer should resemble one of the following (three BRIEF sentences are also acceptable):

> "The Fox played a trick on the Stork, so the Stork played the same trick on the Fox. The moral of the story was that you shouldn't play tricks unless you can put up with tricks played on you."

"The Fox thought the Stork was funny looking, so he invited the Stork to dinner. But the soup was served in a shallow dish, and the Stork couldn't eat it. So the Stork played the same trick on the Fox."

"The Fox invited the Stork to dinner and fed him soup in a dish that was too shallow for the Stork to eat from. So the Stork invited the Fox to dinner and gave him fish in a jar with a narrow top."

Write down the student's narration as he watches. Then, choose one of the sentences from the narration to use as a dictation exercise. Follow the same dictation techniques as above.

WEEKS 2–10

Follow the same pattern as above:

DAY ONE: Narration Exercise

Choose readings of about four paragraphs, or 16 to 20 lines; after asking the student questions to test comprehension, help the student identify the most important elements of the story before asking, "Can you tell me in two sentences what happened in this story?"

DAY TWO: Copywork

Choose copywork sentences of ten to twelve words. Over this nine-week period, look for sentences with the following grammatical elements. Point the elements out in each sentence before the student copies.

Action verbs, the pronoun I (capitalized) .... Week 2
Linking verbs .... Week 3
Commands and questions .... Week 4
Names of the seasons .... Week 5
Commas in dates .... Week 6
Commas in addresses .... Week 7
Commas in a series....................................... Weeks 8–10

If you cannot find sentences that contain these elements, alternate choosing copywork sentences from the student's books and making up your own copywork sentences with these elements included; this will help the student to practice proper form.

DAY THREE: Dictation

Dictate the sentence used for copywork the day before.

DAY FOUR: Narration Exercise and Dictation

Choose readings of about four paragraphs, or 16 to 20 lines; after asking the student questions to test comprehension, help the student identify the most important elements of the story before asking, "Can you tell me in two sentences what happened in this story?" Write down the student's narration as he watches. Then, choose one of the sentences from the narration to use as a dictation exercise. Follow the same dictation techniques as above.

Year Two, Weeks 11–18

Copywork sentences will still be used for dictation, but their length will grow to 12 to 15 words, further developing the student's memory; the sentences will introduce helping verbs, contractions, adjectives, interjections, conjunctions, and direct quotations. Narration passages will expand to five paragraphs, or around 20 to 22 lines (these are only general guidelines, since shorter passages can be denser and more difficult to remember than passages containing many short lines of dialogue). Narration sentences will be used for dictation, but the student will not look at them first.

The pattern established in Week 11 will be followed in Weeks 12 through 18.

WEEK 11

DAY ONE: Narration Exercise

Although the following passage comes from a novel, it is descriptive rather than narrative; instead of asking the student what happened, you will use the comprehension questions to identify important details. This will begin to train the student to understand the structure of expository writing.

Explain to the student that this passage is from the original book *The 101 Dalmatians*, written by Dodie Smith; the Disney version was a very simplified retelling of this wonderful story. This scene takes place near the beginning of the book; Mr. and Mrs. Dearly, owners of the Dalmatian dogs Pongo and Missis, are taking a walk with their dogs when they meet Mrs. Dearly's old friend Cruella de Vil.

> It was a beautiful September evening, windless, very peaceful. The park and the old, cream-painted houses facing it basked in the golden light of sunset. There were many sounds but no noises. The cries of playing children and the whir of London's traffic seemed quieter than usual, as if softened by the evening's gentleness. Birds were singing their last song of the day, and farther along the Circle, at the house where a great composer lived, someone was playing the piano.
>
> "I shall always remember this happy walk," said Mr. Dearly.

At that moment the peace was shattered by an extremely strident motor horn. A large car was coming towards them. It drew up at a big house just ahead of them, and a tall woman came out onto the front-door steps. She was wearing a tight-fighting emerald satin dress, several ropes of rubies, and an absolutely simple white mink cloak, which reached to the high heels of her ruby-red shoes. She had a dark skin, black eyes with a tinge of red in them, and a very pointed nose. Her hair was parted severely down the middle and one half of it was black and the other white—rather unusual.

"Why, that's Cruella de Vil," said Mrs. Dearly. "We were at school together. She was expelled for drinking ink."

"Isn't she a bit showy?" said Mr. Dearly, and would have turned back. But the tall woman had seen Mrs. Dearly and come down the steps to meet her. So Mrs. Dearly had to introduce Mr. Dearly.

"Come and meet *my* husband," said the tall woman.

"But you were going out," said Mrs. Dearly, looking at the chauffeur who was waiting at the open door of the large car. It was painted black and white, in stripes—rather noticeable.

—From *The 101 Dalmatians*
by Dodie Smith

Ask the following questions to test the student's listening ability. If the student cannot remember the details, reread the section of the passage that answers the question.

Instructor: In what month does the story take place?
Student: The story happens in September.

Instructor: In the first part of the story, four different sounds are mentioned. Can you remember two of them?
Student: Playing children were making noise; traffic was whirring; birds were singing; someone was playing the piano.

Instructor: What kind of noise shattered the peace?

Student: *The noise of a motor horn shattered the peace.*

Instructor: Can you remember two of the four things that Cruella de Vil was wearing?
Student: *She was wearing an emerald satin dress, rubies, a mink cloak, and ruby red shoes.*

Instructor: What was unusual about Cruella's hair?
Student: *It was half black and half white.*

Instructor: How about her eyes?
Student: *They had a red tinge.*

Instructor: Why was Cruella expelled from school?
Student: *She drank ink.*

Instructor: What did Cruella's car look like?
Student: *Her car had black and white stripes.*

Now ask the student, "Can you describe the most important things about Cruella de Vil in one or two sentences?" The description should mention at least one of the odd things about her—the color of her hair, and the red tint in her eyes. Encourage the student to list *only* details that are in the passages, and not details that he may have seen in a movie version. If the student points out that "de Vil" sounds like "devil," that is acceptable (since it can be deduced from the passage).

Acceptable answers might sound like one of the following:

"Cruella de Vil was a very tall woman in a mink cloak. She had red eyes, and her hair was half black and half white."

"Cruella de Vil had a pointed nose and black-and-white hair. She was wearing a satin dress and rubies."

"Cruella de Vil had red shoes and red eyes. Her hair was black and white, and so was her car."

Write down the student's narration as he watches.

DAY TWO: Copywork

Copy out the following sentences on second-grade lined paper, in neat print handwriting, for the student to copy. Tell the student that these sentences come from a little later in the book *101 Dalmatians*; Cruella de Vil has invited the two Dearlys for dinner, but all the food tastes like pepper.

Remind the student that the copied sentences should look exactly like the original. Point out that there are three kinds of ending punctuation here—a period following the statement, a question mark following the question, and an exclamation point following the one-word exclamatory answer to the question. "Pepper!" is not a complete sentence; answering a question is one of the instances in which it is correct to use a fragment in writing.

> The soup was dark purple. And what did it taste of? Pepper!

DAY THREE: Dictation

Dictate the sentences above to the student twice. Ask him if he can remember the punctuation without looking at it. When you read the sentences, use a flat tone for the first statement, a questioning voice for the second question, and an excited voice for "Pepper!" If the student begins to write the wrong ending punctuation, gently correct him.

DAY FOUR: Narration Exercise and Dictation

Before reading this passage to the student, tell him that Missis and Pongo have already had their puppies. Cruella de Vil comes to see them while the puppies are playing in the "area"—the little fenced courtyard just outside the door to their house. Nanny Butler, who is Mr. Dearly's old nurse, and Nanny Cook, who is Mrs. Dearly's old nurse, are watching the puppies, when they see Cruella de Vil approaching. Lucky, the most adventuresome puppy, has a horseshoe pattern of spots on his back; that's where he gets his nickname.

> Cruella opened the gate and walked down the steps, saying how pretty the puppies were. Lucky, always the ringleader, came running towards her and nibbled at the fur round the tops of her boots. She picked him up and placed him against

her cloak, as if he were something to be worn.

"Such a pretty horseshoe," she said, looking at the spots on his back. "But they all have pretty markings. Are they old enough to leave their mother yet?"

"Very nearly," said Nanny Butler. "But they won't have to. Mr. and Mrs. Dearly are going to keep them *all*." (Sometimes the Nannies wondered just how this was going to be managed.)

"How nice!" said Cruella, and began going up the steps, still holding Lucky against her cloak. Pongo, Missis, and Perdita all barked sharply, and Lucky reached up and nipped Cruella's ear. She gave a scream and dropped him. Nanny Butler was quick enough to catch him in her apron.

"That woman!" said Nanny Cook, who had just come out into the area. "She's enough to frighten the spots off a pup. What's the matter, Lucky?"

For Lucky had dashed into the laundry and was gulping down water. Cruella's ear had tasted of pepper.

—From *The 101 Dalmatians*
by Dodie Smith

Ask the following questions to test the student's listening ability. Remind the student to answer in complete sentences; if he answers in a fragment, put the answer in the form of a sentence and then require the student to repeat it back to you.

Instructor: Which puppy ran forward to greet Cruella?
Student: Lucky ran to greet her.

Instructor: What markings did Lucky have on his back?
Student: He had a horseshoe on his back.

Instructor: When Cruella picked Lucky up, where did she hold him?
Student: She held him against her cloak as if she wanted to wear him.

Instructor: What are the names of the two nannies in the

passage?
Student: *They are Nanny Cook and Nanny Butler.*

Instructor: How did Lucky get out of Cruella's arms?
Student: *He nipped her ear.*

Instructor: What did she taste like?
Student: *She tasted like pepper.*

Instructor: What do you think Cruella was trying to do with Lucky?
Student: *She was trying to kidnap him.* (Prompt the student for this answer if necessary.)

You will now continue to teach the student to summarize the basic narrative thread in the passage. In order to do this, say to the student:

Instructor: What were the puppies doing when Cruella arrived?
Student: *They were playing in the "area."*

Instructor: What did she do then?
Student: *She picked Lucky up.*

Instructor: Did she put him down right away?
Student: *No.*

Instructor: What did she do instead?
Student: *She walked away with him.*

Instructor: How did Lucky get free?
Student: *Lucky nipped Cruella's ear.*

Now ask the student, "Can you tell me in two sentences what happened in this story?" The student's answer should resemble one of the following (three BRIEF sentences are also acceptable):

"Cruella de Vil saw the puppies playing. She picked Lucky up and tried to take him away. He nipped her ear and got away from her."

"Cruella de Vil tried to steal Lucky, but he bit her ear and got away. Her ear tasted like pepper."

"Cruella de Vil came to see whether the puppies were ready to leave their mother. She tried to take Lucky, but he escaped from her."

Write down the student's narration, but do not allow him to see the sentences. Choose one of the sentences from the narration to use as a dictation exercise. Be sure to indicate any unusual punctuation with your voice; give any necessary spelling help.

WEEKS 12–18

DAY ONE: Narration Exercise
Increase the length of narrated passages to around five paragraphs. Choose a mixture of story passages and descriptive passages. Ask the student comprehension questions before requiring her to give a narration. For stories, ask the student to tell what happened; for descriptive passages, ask her to identify the most important details. Write the student's narration down as she watches.

DAY TWO: Copywork
Increase the length of copywork sentences to 12 to 15 words. Introduce the following elements, pointing them out to the student before she begins to copy.

Helping verbs .... Week 12
Contractions and direct quotations .... Weeks 13–14
Adjectives .... Week 15
Predicate adjectives .... Week 16
Interjections .... Week 17
Conjunctions .... Week 18

If you cannot find sentences that contain these elements, alternate choosing copywork sentences from the student's books and making up your own copywork sentences with these elements included; this will help the student to practice proper form.

DAY THREE: Dictation

Use the copywork sentence from the previous day as a dictation exercise, repeating the sentence twice before the student writes.

DAY FOUR: Narration Exercise and Dictation

Follow the principles outlined in Day One. Write the student's narration down, but do not allow her to watch. Choose one of the sentences from the narration and dictate it back to the student, giving all necessary help.

Predicate Adjective follows a linking verb and modifies the subject of the l.v.

Year Two, Weeks 19–27

Copywork sentences will still be used for dictation, but will include dialogue and more than one sentence. Narration passages will remain at around five paragraphs; narration sentences will be used for dictation, but the student will not examine them first.

The pattern established in Week 19 will be followed in Weeks 20 through 27.

WEEK 19

DAY ONE: Narration Exercise

Tell the student that the following passage is from a book called *Five Children and It*, by Edith Nesbit. Five children have been sent to live in the English countryside near the sea while their mother is away. They are looked after by a nanny named Martha, but for most of every day, they have to entertain themselves. One day, they are out digging in the sand near the sea when they discover a sand-fairy—a magical prehistoric creature called the Psammead who can grant wishes. Unfortunately, their wishes don't usually turn out as they expect.

In the day before this scene, the five children wished for boundless wealth—and the fairy gave them old-fashioned pieces of gold that no one would take for money. They have decided that they are going to talk the problem over at breakfast and decide what to wish for next, but they have to feed their baby brother breakfast while they're talking. Cyril is the oldest brother; "Panther" is the children's nickname for Anthea, the oldest sister; and the baby's nickname is "the Lamb."

> There was no chance of talking things over before breakfast, because everyone overslept itself, as it happened, and it needed a vigorous and determined struggle to get dressed so as to be only ten minutes late for breakfast. During this meal some efforts were made to deal with the question of the Psammead in an impartial spirit, but it is very difficult to discuss anything thoroughly and at the same time to attend faithfully to your baby brother's breakfast needs. The Baby was particularly lively that morning. He not only wriggled his

body through the bar of his high chair, and hung by his head,
choking and purple, but he seized a tablespoon with desperate
suddenness, hit Cyril heavily on the head with it, and then
cried because it was taken away from him. He put his fat fist
in his bread-and-milk, and demanded "nam [jam]," which was
only allowed for tea. He sang, he put his feet on the table—he
clamoured to "go walky." The conversation was something like
this—

"Look here—about that Sand-fairy—Look out!—he'll have
the milk over."

Milk removed to a safe distance.

"Yes—about that Fairy—No, Lamb dear, give Panther the
narky poon."

Then Cyril tried. "Nothing we've had yet has turned out—
He nearly had the mustard that time!"

"I wonder whether we'd better wish—Hullo!—you've done
it now, my boy!" And in a flash of glass and pink baby-paws,
the bowl of golden carp in the middle of the table rolled on its
side and poured a flood of mixed water and gold-fish into the
Baby's lap and into the laps of the others.

Everyone was almost as much upset as the gold-fish; the
Lamb only remaining calm. When the pool on the floor had
been mopped up, and the leaping, gasping gold-fish had been
collected and put back in the water, the Baby was taken away
to be entirely re-dressed by Martha, and most of the others had
to change completely.

—From *Five Children and It*
by Edith Nesbit

You will use comprehension questions to help the student recall
important details; if the student cannot remember, reread the section of the
passage that answers the question.

Instructor: Why did the children have trouble talking to
each other about the sand-fairy?
Student: *The baby kept distracting them.*

Instructor: What happened when the baby tried to wiggle out of his high chair?
Student: *He got caught by the head and turned purple.*

Instructor: What did he do with the tablespoon?
Student: *He hit Cyril with it.*

Instructor: What did he do when the tablespoon was taken away?
Student: *He cried.*

Instructor: What did he knock over?
Student: *He knocked over the goldfish bowl in the center of the table.*

Instructor: What did the other children have to do then?
Student: *They had to change their clothes completely.*

Instructor: Can you list two more annoying things the baby did at breakfast?
Student: *He put his fist in his bread and milk; he sang; he put his feet on the table; he asked to go for a walk; he asked for jam.*

Now ask the student, "Can you describe three annoying things the baby did at breakfast—two small things and one large thing?" The "large thing" should be the knocking over of the goldfish bowl. The other two actions can be any of the details highlighted in the comprehension questions.

The narration can be three brief sentences, or two longer sentences. Write down the student's narration as he watches.

Day Two: Copywork

Explain to the student that, after breakfast, the children were setting out to find the sand-fairy when Martha, the nanny, ordered them to take the baby with them. They objected that they didn't want him, but Martha said, "Not want him indeed! Everybody wants him, the duck!"

So the children took him to the sandy place where the fairy lived, but he got sand in his eyes, threw sand at Anthea, and knocked over their drinks.

The younger brother, Robert, was so upset that he shouted, "I only wish everybody did want him...we might get some peace in our lives!" But the sand-fairy had appeared, without their realizing it, and was sitting behind them. Here is what it said:

> "Good morning," it said. "I did that quite easily! Everyone wants him now."

Copy this sentence out on second-grade lined paper. Put it in front of the student. Before he begins to copy, point out that quotation marks surround the exact words spoken by the sand-fairy; that there is a comma between the first part of the sand-fairy's speech and the words that tell you who said it ("it said"—this is called a *dialogue tag*); that there is a period after "*it said*"; that the second part of the sand-fairy's speech is an exclamation and ends with an exclamation point; and that the last period of the speech goes *inside* the closing quotation mark.

DAY THREE: Dictation
Use the copywork sentence from the previous day as a dictation exercise, repeating the sentence twice before the student writes. Remind the student of the correct punctuation before he begins to write.

DAY FOUR: Narration Exercise and Dictation
Tell the student that this passage is a little story, and that after you read it out loud, you will ask him to tell you what happened. Explain that the sand-fairy has granted Robert's wish—now, everyone they meet will want the baby. They decide they should go home immediately!

> At the gate into the road the party stopped to shift the Lamb from Cyril's back to Robert's. And as they paused a very smart open carriage came in sight, with a coachman and a groom on the box, and inside the carriage a lady—very grand indeed, with a dress all white lace and red ribbons and a parasol all red and white—and a white fluffy dog on her lap with a red ribbon round its neck. She looked at the children, and particularly at the Baby, and she smiled at him. The children were used to this, for the Lamb was, as all the servants said, a

"very taking child." So they waved their hands politely to the lady and expected her to drive on. But she did not. Instead she made the coachman stop. And she beckoned to Cyril, and when he went up to the carriage she said, "What a dear darling duck of a baby! Oh, I *should* so like to adopt it! Do you think its mother would mind?"

"She'd mind very much indeed," said Anthea shortly.

"Oh, but I should bring it up in luxury, you know. I am Lady Chittenden. You must have seen my photograph in the illustrated papers. They call me a Beauty, you know, but of course that's all nonsense. Anyway"—

She opened the carriage door and jumped out. She had the wonderfullest red high-heeled shoes with silver buckles. "Let me hold him a minute," she said. And she took the Lamb and held him very awkwardly, as if she was not used to babies.

Then suddenly she jumped into the carriage with the Lamb in her arms and slammed the door, and said, "Drive on!"

The Lamb roared, the little white dog barked, and the coachman hesitated.

"Drive on, I tell you!" cried the lady; and the coachman did, for, as he said afterwards, it was as much as his place was worth not to.

The four children looked at each other, and then with one accord they rushed after the carriage and held on behind. Down the dusty road went the smart carriage, and after it, at double-quick time, ran the twinkling legs of the Lamb's brothers and sisters.

—From *Five Children and It*
by Edith Nesbit

Ask the following questions to test the student's listening ability. Remind the student to answer in complete sentences; if he answers in a fragment, put the answer in the form of a sentence and then require the student to repeat it back to you.

Instructor: What were the children doing while they were standing at the gate?
Student: They were moving the baby from one back to another—he was riding piggyback.

Instructor: Why did the children expect the lady dressed in white to "move on" after she smiled at the baby?
Student: They were used to people smiling at the baby.

Instructor: What did the lady ask the children?
Student: She asked whether she could adopt the baby.

Instructor: What did the lady do then?
Student: She got out of her carriage to hold the baby.

Instructor: Did she seem comfortable with babies?
Student: No, she held him awkwardly.

Instructor: Why do you think she wanted the baby?
Student: The sand-fairy's magic made her want the baby.
(Prompt the student for this answer if necessary.)

Instructor: What did the lady do as soon as she had the baby in her arms?
Student: She jumped in her carriage and told her coachman to drive away.

Instructor: What did the children do?
Student: They ran after her.

You will now continue to teach the student to summarize the basic narrative thread in the passage. In order to do this, say to the student:

Instructor: What were the children doing when the lady drove by?
Student: They were standing at the gate, giving the baby a piggyback.

Instructor: What did the lady do when she got out of the carriage?

Student: *She took the baby and drove away.* (If the student only answers with "She took the baby," ask, "What then?")

Instructor: What did the children do?
Student: *They ran after her.*

Now ask the student, "Can you tell me in two sentences what happened in this story? Make sure to tell me why the lady wanted the baby." The student's answer should resemble one of the following:

> "The fairy's magic made everyone want the baby. A lady in a carriage grabbed him and took him away, but the children ran after her."

> "After the sand-fairy granted a wish, everyone wanted the baby. The children were standing at a gate when a lady in a carriage stopped and smiled at the baby. She held him, and then she jumped in her carriage and drove away."

> "A lady in a carriage stole the baby because she wanted him. She was actually awkward with babies, but the sand-fairy's magic was affecting her."

Write down the student's narration, but do not allow him to see the sentences. Choose one of the sentences from the narration to use as a dictation exercise. Be sure to indicate any unusual punctuation with your voice; give any necessary spelling help.

WEEKS 20–27

DAY ONE: Narration Exercise

Narration passages should remain around five paragraphs in length. Choose a mixture of story passages and descriptive passages. Ask the student comprehension questions before requiring the student to give a narration. For stories, ask the student to tell what happened; for descriptive passages, ask the student to identify the most important details. Write the student's narration down as he watches.

DAY TWO: Copywork

Choose copywork from history, literature, or science; selections should be around 12 to 15 words (or longer if the student's writing ability permits), ideally two short sentences. Make an effort to look for selections that include dialogue, so that the student can practice correct punctuation; also, make an effort to have more than one sentence in the selections as often as possible.

Introduce the following elements, pointing them out to the student before he begins to copy.

Direct quotations and indirect quotations .... Weeks 20–23
Adverbs .... Weeks 24–25
Titles of Respect .... Weeks 26–27

If you cannot find sentences that contain these elements, alternate choosing copywork sentences from the student's books and making up your own copywork sentences with these elements included; this will help the student to practice proper form.

DAY THREE: Dictation

Use the copywork sentence from the previous day as a dictation exercise, repeating the sentence twice before the student writes. Remind the student of the correct punctuation before he begins to write.

DAY FOUR: Narration Exercise and Dictation

Follow the principles outlined in Day One; if the Day One passage was focused on description, choose a narrative passage (or vice versa). Write the student's narration down, but do not allow him to watch. Choose one of the sentences from the narration and dictate it back to the student, giving all necessary help.

Year Two, Weeks 28–35

During this final step of Year Two, dictation will replace copywork. The student will take dictation sentences of 12 to 15 words that have not been copied first. Narration passages will grow slightly longer, to five or six paragraphs or 26 to 29 lines (these are only general guidelines, since shorter passages can be denser and more difficult to remember than passages containing many short lines of dialogue). The student will be encouraged to answer the more general question "Can you give me a short summary of this passage?" rather than the more specific questions used earlier (this will require the student to decide whether the narration calls for a retelling of the story, or a listing of important details).

The pattern established in Week 28 will be followed in Weeks 29 through 35.

WEEK 28

DAY ONE: Narration Exercise

Tell the student that this passage is from a book called *The Magic of Oz*, by the writer L. Frank Baum, who wrote *The Wonderful Wizard of Oz* and then wrote many other books about Dorothy and her friends in Oz and the magical countries that surround it.

In this story, two friends—a little girl named Trot and a sailor named Cap'n Bill—have sailed off on an expedition, accompanied by an enchanted cat made out of glass. They are trying to find a birthday present for the ruler of Oz, a beautiful princess named Ozma who already has everything she could possibly want. But Trot and Cap'n Bill have heard about a Magic Flower that blooms constantly, with all kinds of different blossoms. It grows on a deserted island in a golden pot, and Trot and Cap'n Bill have just arrived at the deserted island and seen the flower.

> So intently did Trot and Cap'n Bill gaze upon the Golden Flowerpot that held the Magic Flower that they scarcely noticed the island itself until the raft beached upon its sands. But then the girl exclaimed: "How funny it is, Cap'n Bill, that nothing else grows here except the Magic Flower."
>
> Then the sailor glanced at the island and saw that it was all bare ground, without a weed, a stone, or a blade of grass. Trot,

eager to examine the Flower closer, sprang from the raft and ran up the bank until she reached the Golden Flowerpot. Then she stood beside it motionless and filled with wonder. Cap'n Bill joined her, coming more leisurely, and he, too, stood in silent admiration for a time.

"Ozma will like this," remarked the Glass Cat, sitting down to watch the shifting hues of the flowers. "I'm sure she won't have as fine a birthday present from anyone else."

"Do you 'spose it's very heavy, Cap'n? And can we get it home without breaking it?" asked Trot anxiously.

"Well, I've lifted many bigger things than that," he replied; "but let's see what it weighs."

He tried to take a step forward, but could not lift his meat foot from the ground. His wooden leg seemed free enough, but the other would not budge.

"I seem stuck, Trot," he said, with a perplexed look at his foot. "It ain't mud, an' it ain't glue, but somethin's holdin' me down."

The girl attempted to lift her own feet, to go nearer to her friend, but the ground held them as fast as it held Cap'n Bill's foot. She tried to slide them, or to twist them around, but it was no use; she could not move either foot a hair's breadth.

"This is funny!" she exclaimed. "What do you 'spose has happened to us, Cap'n Bill?"

"I'm tryin' to make out," he answered. "Take off your shoes, Trot. P'raps it's the leather soles that's stuck to the ground." She leaned down and unlaced her shoes, but found she could not pull her feet out of them. The Glass Cat, which was walking around as naturally as ever, now said:

"Your foot has got roots to it, Cap'n, and I can see the roots going into the ground, where they spread out in all directions. It's the same way with Trot. That's why you can't move. The roots hold you fast."

—From *The Magic of Oz*
by L. Frank Baum.

After asking the student the following comprehension questions, you'll ask her the general question "Can you give me a brief summary of this passage?" The student should respond by telling you what *happens* in the story, rather than with a listing of details. The comprehension questions are designed to guide the student towards recognizing the need for a plot summary.

Test the student's comprehension with these questions:

> **Instructor:** What odd thing did Trot notice about the island?
> **Student:** *Nothing else grew there.*

> **Instructor:** What happened when Cap'n Bill tried to step forward and lift the pot?
> **Student:** *His foot stuck to the ground.*

> **Instructor:** Did both feet stick to the ground?
> **Student:** *No, his wooden foot was free.*

> **Instructor:** What happened when Trot tried to help him?
> **Student:** *She found out that her feet were stuck too.*

> **Instructor:** Did taking off her shoes help?
> **Student:** *No, her feet were still stuck.*

> **Instructor:** The Glass Cat could see the problem. What was it?
> **Student:** *Their feet had grown roots.*

> **Instructor:** Why do you think the Glass Cat's feet and the wooden leg didn't grow roots?
> **Student:** *Only living things grew roots.* (Prompt the student for this answer if necessary.)

Now ask the student for a summary of the passage in two or three brief sentences. Her answer should resemble one of the following:

> "Trot and Cap'n Bill came to the island to get the Magic Flower for Ozma. But their feet grew roots so that they couldn't move."

"The Magic Flower grew on a deserted island. Trot and Cap'n Bill came to the island to get the flower. When they stepped on the island, their feet grew roots."

"Trot and Cap'n Bill came to get the Magic Flower. When they stepped on the island where it grew, their feet grew roots. The Glass Cat's feet didn't grow roots, so it could still walk around."

If the student has difficulty forming a brief summary, ask these three questions:

Why did Trot and Cap'n Bill come to the island?
What happened when they stepped onto the island?
Did the same thing happen to the Glass Cat?

Then, have the student repeat her answers in order; this will form her brief summary.

Write the student's narration down as she watches.

DAY TWO: Dictation

Tell the student that, since the Glass Cat was not caught by the magic island, it set off to find help for Trot and Cap'n Bill. Then repeat the following sentence twice. Ask the student to repeat it back to you before writing. Point out that, in terms of this book, the writer uses "Glass Cat" as a proper name, so both words should be capitalized.

"Travelled" can also be spelled "traveled."

It was a wild country and little travelled, but the Glass Cat knew every path.

DAY THREE: Dictation

Tell the student that the dictation sentences today are about the Glass Cat. Here is the beginning of the description of the Glass Cat: "This astonishing cat was made all of glass and was so clear and transparent that you could see through it as easily as through a window. In the top of its head, however, was a mass of delicate pink balls which looked like jewels but were intended for brains."

Then repeat the following sentences twice. Ask the student to repeat them back to you before writing. Be sure to emphasize the end of the first sentence with your voice. Also, tell the student that "blood-red" is a compound adjective (two adjectives together) connected by a hyphen.

> It had a heart made of a blood-red ruby. The eyes were two large emeralds.

DAY FOUR: Narration Exercise and Dictation

This scene comes a little later in *The Magic of Oz*. Trot and Cap'n Bill have been standing on the island a very long time, waiting for rescue. They are both getting tired and hungry.

Trot sighed again and watched the wonderful Magic Flower, because there was nothing else to do. Just now a lovely group of pink peonies budded and bloomed, but soon they faded away, and a mass of deep blue lilies took their place. Then some yellow chrysanthemums blossomed on the plant, and when they had opened all their petals and reached perfection, they gave way to a lot of white floral balls spotted with crimson—a flower Trot had never seen before.

"But I get awful tired watchin' flowers an' flowers an' flowers," she said impatiently.

"They're mighty pretty," observed Cap'n Bill.

"I know; and if a person could come and look at the Magic Flower just when she felt like it, it would be a fine thing, but to HAVE TO stand and watch it, whether you want to or not, isn't so much fun. I wish, Cap'n Bill, the thing would grow fruit for a while instead of flowers."

Scarcely had she spoken when the white balls with crimson spots faded away and a lot of beautiful ripe peaches took their place. With a cry of mingled surprise and delight Trot reached out and plucked a peach from the bush and began to eat it, finding it delicious. Cap'n Bill was somewhat dazed at the girl's wish being granted so quickly, so before he could pick a peach they had faded away and bananas took their place. "Grab one,

Cap'n!" exclaimed Trot, and even while eating the peach she seized a banana with her other hand and tore it from the bush.

The old sailor was still bewildered. He put out a hand indeed, but he was too late, for now the bananas disappeared and lemons took their place.

"Pshaw!" cried Trot. "You can't eat those things; but watch out, Cap'n, for something else."

Cocoanuts next appeared, but Cap'n Bill shook his head.

"Can't crack 'em," he remarked, "'cause we haven't anything handy to smash 'em with."

"Well, take one, anyhow," advised Trot; but the cocoanuts were gone now, and a deep, purple, pear-shaped fruit which was unknown to them took their place. Again Cap'n Bill hesitated, and Trot said to him:

"You ought to have captured a peach and a banana, as I did. If you're not careful, Cap'n, you'll miss all your chances. Here, I'll divide my banana with you."

Even as she spoke, the Magic Plant was covered with big red apples, growing on every branch, and Cap'n Bill hesitated no longer. He grabbed with both hands and picked two apples, while Trot had only time to secure one before they were gone.

—From *The Magic of Oz*
by L. Frank Baum

After asking the student the following comprehension questions, you'll ask her the general question "Can you give me a brief summary of this passage?" The student should respond by giving you the important details about the Magic Plant, rather than telling you what *happens* in the story. The comprehension questions are designed to guide the student towards recognizing the need to list important details.

Test the student's comprehension with these questions:

Instructor: Can you list two of the four kinds of flowers that blossom on the Magic Flower while Trot watches?
Student: *There were pink peonies, blue lilies, yellow chrysanthemums, and white balls with crimson (a kind of*

flower Trot didn't know the name of).

Instructor: After Trot wished that the Magic Flower would bear fruit, it instantly produced two kinds of fruit. Can you remember one of them?
Student: *It had peaches and bananas.*

Instructor: What two kinds of fruit did Trot and Cap'n Bill decide *not* to pick?
Student: *They didn't pick lemons or coconuts.* (Note that the passage uses an archaic alternate spelling.)

Instructor: After the strange purple fruit, what did the Magic Flower bear?
Student: *It grew big red apples.*

Now ask the student for two or three brief sentences summarizing the passage. Her answer should focus on the details in the passage; if she can't remember the details, read part of the paragraph to her again. Her answer should contain at least three different specific details of fruit and flowers, plus the information that the flower could have both. For example:

"The Magic Flower had all kinds of blossoms, like pink peonies and blue lilies. When Trot wished that it would have fruit instead, peaches, bananas, coconuts, and apples grew on it."

"Trot was tired of flowers and wished for fruit. The Magic Flower had peaches, bananas, and apples. It also had lemons and coconuts, but Trot and Cap'n Bill didn't eat those."

"The Magic Flower could have fruit as well as flowers. Trot picked peaches and bananas from it, and Cap'n Bill picked apples."

Write down the student's narration, but do not allow her to watch. Then dictate one of the sentences back to her. Remind her that Magic Flower is capitalized because the writer treats it like a proper name. Cap'n is also capitalized because it is part of Cap'n Bill's proper name.

WEEKS 29–35

Follow the same pattern as above:

DAY ONE: Narration Exercise

Increase the length of narrated passages to around five or six paragraphs, as above. Alternate passages with a strong storyline that need retelling, and passages with description that require the student to remember and repeat details. Ask the student comprehension questions before asking for a brief, two- to three-sentence summary. Write the student's narration down as he watches.

DAYS TWO AND THREE: Dictation

Dictate selections of 12 to 15 words that the student has not yet seen; try to alternate between two shorter sentences and one longer sentence.

Repeat the selection twice, indicating dialogue or unusual punctuation with your voice. Have the student repeat the selection back to you before writing. You may prompt the student one additional time, if necessary, but encourage him to think first.

Over these seven weeks, look for selections that include the following elements. Point them out to the student after he writes.

Articles .... Week 29
Prepositions .... Weeks 30–31
Synonyms .... Weeks 32–33
Antonyms .... Weeks 34–35

If you cannot find sentences that contain these elements, alternate choosing dictation sentences from the student's books and making up your own dictation sentences with these elements included; this will help the student to practice proper form.

DAY FOUR: Narration Exercise and Dictation

Follow the narration guidelines above. Write the student's narration down, but do not allow him to watch; use 12 to 15 words of the narration as the final dictation exercise of the week.

Year Two Mastery Evaluation, Week 36

Before moving to Year Three, the student should be able to take one long (12 to 15 words) or two short sentences from dictation, after two repetitions. He should also be able to answer questions about a passage of five to six paragraphs, and then to summarize the passage in a two- to three-sentence narration. Finally, he should be able to take a sentence of his own narration down as a dictation exercise.

Use the following assignments to evaluate the student's mastery of these skills; you may do these over several days or all at once, depending on the student's maturity.

If the student still struggles with narration or dictation, spend a few more weeks on these skills before moving on.

Narration Evaluation

This passage is from the novel *Peter Pan*, by J. M. Barrie. Peter Pan has come to visit the three Darling children, Wendy, John, and the youngest child, Michael, while their parents and their nurse, Nana, are at a dinner party next door. Peter Pan wants the three children to come back to Neverland with him. He tells them that they can fly to Neverland if they just have wonderful thoughts—but even while they are thinking wonderful thoughts, they can't get off the ground.

> Of course Peter had been trifling with them, for no one can fly unless the fairy dust has been blown on him. Fortunately, as we have mentioned, one of his hands was messy with it, and he blew some on each of them, with the most superb results.
>
> "Now just wiggle your shoulders this way," he said, "and let go."
>
> They were all on their beds, and gallant Michael let go first. He did not quite mean to let go, but he did it, and immediately he was borne across the room.
>
> "I flewed!" he screamed while still in mid-air.
>
> John let go and met Wendy near the bathroom.
>
> "Oh, lovely!"
>
> "Oh, ripping!"
>
> "Look at me!"
>
> "Look at me!"

"Look at me!"

They were not nearly so elegant as Peter, they could not help kicking a little, but their heads were bobbing against the ceiling, and there is almost nothing so delicious as that. Peter gave Wendy a hand at first, but had to desist, Tink was so indignant.

Up and down they went, and round and round. Heavenly was Wendy's word.

"I say," cried John, "why shouldn't we all go out?"

Of course it was to this that Peter had been luring them.

Michael was ready: he wanted to see how long it took him to do a billion miles. But Wendy hesitated.

"Mermaids!" said Peter again.

"Oo!"

"And there are pirates."

"Pirates," cried John, seizing his Sunday hat, "let us go at once."

It was just at this moment that Mr. and Mrs. Darling hurried with Nana out of 27. They ran into the middle of the street to look up at the nursery window; and, yes, it was still shut, but the room was ablaze with light, and most heart-gripping sight of all, they could see in shadow on the curtain three little figures in night attire circling round and round, not on the floor but in the air.

Not three figures, four!

In a tremble they opened the street door. Mr. Darling would have rushed upstairs, but Mrs. Darling signed him to go softly. She even tried to make her heart go softly.

Will they reach the nursery in time? If so, how delightful for them, and we shall all breathe a sigh of relief, but there will be no story. On the other hand, if they are not in time, I solemnly promise that it will all come right in the end.

They would have reached the nursery in time had it not been that the little stars were watching them. Once again the stars blew the window open, and that smallest star of all called out:

"*Cave*, Peter!" ["Beware" in Latin]

Then Peter knew that there was not a moment to lose. "Come," he cried imperiously, and soared out at once into the night, followed by John and Michael and Wendy.

Mr. and Mrs. Darling and Nana rushed into the nursery too late.

The birds were flown.

—From *Peter Pan*
by J. M. Barrie

Ask the student the following questions. Remember that he should respond in complete sentences; you may remind him of this, but you shouldn't have to form the complete sentences for him.

Instructor: What else, besides wonderful thoughts, did the children need in order to fly?
Student: *They needed fairy dust.*

Instructor: Where did Peter get his fairy dust?
Student: *It was on his hand.*

Instructor: After fairy dust was blown on them, what did the children have to do to fly?
Student: *They had to wiggle their shoulders.*

Instructor: What were the two things that Peter promised them they would see in Neverland?
Student: *There would be mermaids and pirates.*

Instructor: What did Mr. and Mrs. Darling see when they looked up at the nursery window?
Student: *They saw four figures flying in the air.*

Instructor: Who warned Peter that it was time to go?
Student: *A little star called to him.*

Instructor: What did Peter do at once?
Student: He called the children and flew out into the night.

Instructor: Did Mr. and Mrs. Darling reach the nursery in time?
Student: No, the children were already gone.

Now ask the student, "What happened in this passage?" The narration should resemble one of the following:

> "Peter Pan blew fairy dust on the children so that they could fly. They all flew out of the window to Neverland before their parents could come back."

> "The children thought wonderful thoughts, had fairy dust blown on them, and wiggled their shoulders. Then they could fly. They flew out of the window with Peter Pan."

> "The children were getting ready to fly to Neverland when their parents came home. A star warned Peter, and he led them out of the window before their parents could reach the nursery."

> "Peter Pan taught the children to fly and promised them that they would see mermaids and pirates. All four of them flew out of the window before their parents could get to them."

Write the student's narration down, but do not allow him to watch. Then dictate one of the sentences back to the student. Help him with any difficult spelling, and indicate unusual punctuation with your voice.

DICTATION EVALUATION

Tell the student that these two dictation selections come from Chapter 9 of *Peter Pan*, "The Never Bird." Peter Pan is trapped on a rock by the rising tide, but a bird who has her nest on the rock pushes the nest out for him to use as a raft. She is afraid that he will crush her eggs, but instead he puts her eggs into a top hat.

You may do these selections in two different sessions, if necessary. Be sure to use your voice to indicate the period in the first selection.

111

Peter put the eggs into this hat and set it on the lagoon. It floated beautifully.

At the same moment the bird fluttered down upon the hat and once more sat snugly on her eggs.

—From *Peter Pan*
by J. M. Barrie

Year Three
Third Grade (or Level Three, for Older Writers)

Year Three continues to develop the skills of putting thoughts into words (through narration) and putting words down on paper (through increasingly complex dictation). The student will begin to read narration selections independently, and they will increase from around six paragraphs (approximately 30 to 35 lines) to around nine paragraphs (approximately 45 to 50 lines). The student will move from listening to you dictate a sentence of her narration, to dictating it to herself; this is the last step before independent original writing begins. Dictation sentences will increase in complexity and will grow to three sentences, around 20 words, in length. Students will learn to write them after only two repetitions.

The lessons that follow spell out an entire week's assignments whenever the student progresses from one step to the next. If you wish, you can then follow the pattern of this model work, but choose your own copywork and narration assignments. Alternatively, you can use the Year Three workbook; this provides a full sequence of copywork and narration assignments that introduce the student sequentially to the necessary grammatical elements.

If the student has difficulty reading the selections, you may continue to read out loud.

Year Three, Weeks 1–10

Narration exercises remain around six paragraphs, or approximately 30 to 35 lines (these are only general guidelines, since shorter passages can be denser and more difficult to remember than passages containing many short lines of dialogue). However, the student will read the passage independently before answering comprehension questions; she will then summarize the passage in two or three short sentences. She should try to do this from memory, but she can look back at the passage if she gets completely stuck.

Dictation sentences remain at 12 to 15 words, alternating one long sentence and two short sentences; you will also continue to use narration sentences for dictation.

The pattern of Week 1 will serve as the model for Weeks 2 through 10.

WEEK 1

Day One: Narration

The student should read this passage independently. Make sure that she doesn't turn the page to see the comprehension questions!

● — begin reading ——————————————————————

THE STRAW, THE COAL, AND THE BEAN

This story is a very old fairy tale, written down almost 200 years ago by two brothers named Jacob and Wilhelm Grimm who wanted to collect ancient stories and keep them alive.

In a village there lived a poor old woman, who had gathered together a dish of beans and wanted to cook them. So she made a fire on her hearth, and so that it might burn the quicker, she added a handful of straw. When she was emptying the beans into the pan, one dropped without her observing it, and lay on the ground beside a straw, and soon afterwards a burning coal from the fire leapt down to the two.

Then the straw said, "Friends, where do you come from, and how did you get here?"

The coal replied, "I sprang out of the fire, and if I had not escaped by sheer force, my death would have been certain. I would have been burnt to ashes."

The bean said: "I too have escaped with a whole skin, but if the old woman had got me into the pan, I would have been made into soup without any mercy, like all of the others."

"Nothing good would have happened to me either!" said the straw. "The old woman has destroyed all my brothers in fire and smoke; she seized sixty of them at once, and took their lives. I luckily slipped through her fingers."

"But what are we to do now?" said the coal.

"I think," answered the bean, "that since we have so fortunately escaped death, we should keep together like good companions, and go on a journey to a foreign country."

The coal and the straw agreed, and the three set out on their way together. Soon, however, they came to a little brook, and as there was no bridge, they did not know how they were to get over it.

The straw said: "I will lay myself straight across, and then you can walk over on me as on a bridge." So the straw stretched itself from one bank to the other, and the coal tripped quite boldly on to the newly-built bridge. But when she had reached the middle, and heard the water rushing beneath her, she was afraid. She stood still, and did not dare go any farther. The straw began to burn, broke in two pieces, and fell into the stream. The coal slipped after her, hissed when she got into the water, and breathed her last.

The bean, who had prudently stayed behind on the shore, could not but laugh at the event. She was unable to stop, and laughed so heartily that she burst.

It would have been all over with the bean, but by good fortune a tailor, who was travelling in search of work, sat down to rest by the brook. As he had a kind heart, he pulled out his needle and thread, and sewed her together.

The bean thanked him most prettily. And, because the tailor used black thread, all beans since then have a black seam.

—From *Tales from the Brothers Grimm*
by Jacob and Wilhelm Grimm,
trans. Edgar Taylor and Marian Edwardes;
(some archaic language has been clarified by Susan Wise Bauer)

stop reading ▶■

This fable is a more difficult narrative than the Year Two narratives. Help the student begin to identify the central elements by asking the following questions:

> **Instructor:** How did the bean escape from the old woman?
> **Student:** *It dropped out of the pan.*
>
> **Instructor:** How did the coal escape from the fire?
> **Student:** *It leaped out.*
>
> **Instructor:** What else escapes the fire?
> **Student:** *The straw escapes.*
>
> **Instructor:** What do the bean, the coal, and the straw decide to do together?
> **Student:** *They decide to go on a journey to a foreign country.*
>
> **Instructor:** What was the first obstacle they ran into?
> **Student:** *They came to a brook with no bridge across it.*
>
> **Instructor:** What solution did the straw come up with?
> **Student:** *The straw laid himself across the water.*
>
> **Instructor:** Who tried to cross the straw?
> **Student:** *The coal tried to cross.*
>
> **Instructor:** What happened then?
> **Student:** *The coal burned through the straw and fell into the water.*
>
> **Instructor:** How did the bean react?
> **Student:** *She laughed until she split.*
>
> **Instructor:** Who fixed her?
> **Student:** *A tailor sewed her back together.*

Instructor: This fairy tale is a particular kind of story called a "pourquoi (por-kwa) tale." *Pourquoi* is French for "why," and pourquoi tales give imaginative explanations for *why* something is the way it is. What does this tale try to explain?

Student: *It tries to explain why beans have a black seam.*

Now ask the student to summarize the story in three brief sentences. Her answer should resemble one of the following:

"A coal, a straw, and a bean escaped from an old woman. They set out on a journey, but the straw was burnt, the coal fell into water, and the bean split herself laughing. A tailor sewed up the bean with black thread."

"A coal, a straw, and a bean set out on a journey. When they got to a stream, the straw lay down across it as a bridge. The coal went across the straw, but the straw burned, the coal fell into the water, and the bean burst herself laughing."

"A coal, a straw, and a bean came to a stream. The straw tried to become a bridge, but the coal burned the bridge in half and fell in the water. Then the bean split open laughing."

The student will probably attempt to put too much information into the summary. If she has difficulty condensing the story, ask the following three questions:

Who are the three main characters?
What problem did they run into?
What happened to each one?

Write the student's narration down as she watches.

DAY TWO: Dictation

Tell the student that today's dictation sentence is from another one of the Grimms' fairy tales, called "Little Red Cap." It is one of the earliest versions of the story we now know as "Little Red Riding Hood." If you wish, you can read a version of *Little Red Riding Hood* together after completing this dictation exercise.

Be sure to indicate the commas in the sentence by pausing significantly at each one. Tell the student that, since "Little Red Cap" is used as the girl's proper name, all three words should be capitalized.

Read the sentence twice slowly and then ask the student to repeat it back to you before she writes. If she cannot remember the entire sentence, repeat it a third time.

> The grandmother lived out in the wood, half a mile from the village, and just as Little Red Cap entered the wood, a wolf met her.

DAY THREE: Narration and Dictation

The student should read this passage independently. Make sure that she doesn't turn the page to see the comprehension questions!

If the student is not familiar with the custom of "christening," you may want to explain that this was a church ceremony during which babies were baptized and named.

●— **begin reading** ────────────────────

CAT AND MOUSE IN PARTNERSHIP

This is another of the Grimms' fairy tales.

A cat became friends with a mouse, and the two decided to keep house together.

"We must store up some food for winter," said the cat. The mouse agreed, and together the two bought a little pot of bacon fat. But they did not know where to put it.

Finally, after much thought, the cat said, "We should store it in the church, for no one dares steal anything from there. We will set it beneath the altar, and not touch it until we are really in need of it."

So the pot was placed in safety. But it was not long before the cat had a great yearning for it, and said to the mouse: "My cousin has brought a little son into the world. He is white with brown spots, and I must go to the christening."

"Yes, yes," answered the mouse, "by all means go."

But the cat had no cousin. She went straight to the church, stole to the pot, and licked the top of the fat off. Then she took a walk upon the roofs of the town and stretched herself in the sun, and not until it was evening did she return home.

"Well, here you are again," said the mouse. "What name did they give the child?"

"Top-off," said the cat quite coolly.

"Top-off!" cried the mouse, "that is a very odd and uncommon name."

"It is no worse than Crumb-stealer," said the cat, "which is the name of your own little nephew."

Before long the cat was seized by another fit of yearning. She said to the mouse: "You must do me a favour, and once more manage the house for a day alone. Another cousin of mine has had a child."

The good mouse consented, but the cat crept behind the town walls to the church, and devoured half the pot of fat.

When she went home the mouse inquired, "And what was the child named?"

"Half-done," answered the cat.

"Half-done!" said the mouse. "I've never heard such a name in my life!"

The cat's mouth soon began to water for some more of the fat. "All good things go in threes," said she. "My third cousin has had a child—a beautiful black kitten with white paws. You will let me go to the christening, won't you?"

This time, the cat entirely emptied the pot of fat. When she returned home at night, the mouse at once asked what name had been given to the third child.

"It will not please you more than the others," said the cat. "He is called All-gone."

"All-gone!" cried the mouse, "that is the strangest name of all!"

After this, no one invited the cat to christenings, but when the winter had come and there was no longer anything to be found outside, the mouse thought of their provision, and said: "Come, cat, we will go and eat our pot of fat—we shall enjoy that."

"Yes," answered the cat, "just as much as sticking our tongues out the window."

They set out on their way. When they arrived, the pot of fat was still in its place, but it was empty.

"Alas!" said the mouse, "now I see what has happened! You have eaten it all while you were pretending to see your nephews named! First top off, then half-done, then—"

"One more word," cried the cat, "and I will eat you too!"

But "All-gone" was already on the mouse's lips. She had barely spoken it when the cat sprang on her, seized her, and swallowed her down. In truth, that is the way of the world!

—From *Tales from the Brothers Grimm*
by Jacob and Wilhelm Grimm,
trans. Edgar Taylor and Marian Edwardes

—————————————————————————— **stop reading** ▸■

Ask the student the following comprehension questions:

Instructor: What did the cat and the mouse buy for the winter?
Student: They bought a pot of bacon fat.

Instructor: Where did they decide to keep it?
Student: They kept it in the church.

Instructor: What excuse did the cat give for going out and eating the fat?
Student: She said that she had to go to christenings.

Instructor: How many times did she do this?
Student: She did it three times.

Instructor: She told the mouse that the three babies had three strange names. What were they?
Student: *The names were Top-off, Half-done, and All-gone.*

Instructor: When the mouse found out what the cat had done, what happened?
Student: *The cat ate the mouse.*

Instructor: "That is the way of the world" means that the strong will always take advantage of the weak. In what two ways did the cat take advantage of the mouse?
Student: *She ate the bacon fat that they both bought, and then she ate the mouse.*

Now ask the student to summarize the story in three brief sentences. Her summaries should resemble the following:

> "A cat and a mouse set up house together. They bought a pot of fat for the winter, but the cat pretended to go to christenings and ate the entire thing. When the mouse found out, the cat ate him."

> "A cat and a mouse bought a pot of fat and hid it in a church. The cat told the mouse that she had to go to three christenings. Each time she went out, she ate some of the fat, until it was all gone."

> "The cat told the mouse that she was going to the christenings of three babies. She said that they were named Top-off, Half-done, and All-gone. But she had really eaten the pot of fat—first the top, then half, then the rest of it."

If she has difficulty condensing the story, ask the following three questions:

What did the cat and the mouse do together?
In one sentence, how did the cat trick the mouse?
What happened at the end of the story?

Write the student's narration down, but don't let her see the sentences; choose one or two sentences (about 12 to 15 words) to dictate back to the student.

DAY FOUR: Dictation

Tell the student that this is from the Grimms' fairy tale called "Hansel and Gretel." In "Hansel and Gretel," two children lost in the wood stumble into a clearing—and see a house all made out of candy and cake. They are so hungry that they decide to taste it!

Be sure to indicate where the period is by using your voice. You may need to help the student spell the proper names.

> Hansel broke off a piece of the roof, which was made of cake. Gretel nibbled on a pane of sugar glass.

WEEKS 2–10

Follow the same pattern as above:

DAY ONE: Narration Exercise

Choose reading passages of around six paragraphs or 30 to 35 lines from the student's literature, science, or history texts. After the student reads the passage independently, ask the student comprehension questions before requiring a brief, two- or three-sentence summary. Write the student's narration down as he watches.

DAY TWO: Dictation

Dictate selections of 12 to 15 words that the student has not yet seen; try to alternate between two shorter sentences and one longer sentence.

Repeat the selection twice, indicating dialogue or unusual punctuation with your voice. Have the student repeat the selection back to you before writing. You may prompt the student one additional time, if necessary, but encourage him to think first.

Over these nine weeks, look for selections that include the following elements. Point them out to the student after he writes.

Plural nouns (including nouns that end in s, sh,

If you cannot find sentences that contain these elements, alternate choosing dictation sentences from the student's books and making up your own dictation sentences with these elements included; this will help the student to practice proper form.

DAY THREE: Narration and Dictation
Follow the narration guidelines above. Write the student's narration down, but do not allow him to watch; use 12 to 15 words of the narration as the day's dictation exercise.

DAY FOUR: Dictation
Follow the dictation guidelines above.

Year Three, Weeks 11–19

Narration exercises continue around the same length (the passages below are slightly shorter than those in Week 1 because they do not contain dialogue). The student continues to read the passage independently before answering comprehension questions. He will then provide a brief summary of two to three sentences. He should attempt to do this from memory, but he can look back at the passage if he gets stuck.

Dictation exercises will lengthen to 15 to 18 words of two sentences, taken down after three repetitions; *two* narration sentences will be used for dictation.

The pattern of Week 11 will serve as the model for Weeks 12 through 19.

WEEK 11

DAY ONE: Narration Exercise

Tell the student that today's reading passage comes from the Egyptian story "The Treasure Thief." It is about the great Pharaoh Rameses III, who ruled Egypt around 1182–1151 BC. According to this story, Rameses asked his Master Builder, Horemheb, to built him a pyramid that would keep not only his body, but his treasures, safe. But Horemheb tricked him.

This story was first written down by the Greek historian Herodotus around 425 BC. An English writer named Roger Lancelyn Green took the Greek story and retold it in his book *Tales of Ancient Egypt*. This excerpt is from Green's version.

Allow the student to read the following passage independently.

●— begin reading ———————————————————

"THE TREASURE THIEF"

Under the care of the Master Builder the walls of the new building were reared and a pyramid was built over the whole, leaving a great treasure chamber in the middle. In the entrance he set sliding doors of stone, and others of iron and bronze; and when the untold riches of Pharaoh

Rameses were placed in the chamber, the doors were locked and each was sealed with Pharaoh's great seal, that none might copy on pain of death....

Yet Hor-em-heb the Master Builder played Pharaoh false. In the thick wall of the Treasure House he made a narrow passage, with a stone at either end turning on a pivot that, when closed, looked and felt like any other part of the smooth, strong wall—except for those who knew where to feel for the hidden spring that held it firmly in place.

By means of this secret entrance Hor-em-heb was able to add to the reward which Pharaoh gave to him when the Treasure House was complete. Yet he did not add much, for very soon a great sickness fell upon him, and presently he died.

But on his death-bed he told his two sons about the secret entrance to the Treasure House; and when he was dead, and they had buried his body with all honour in a rock chamber among the Tombs of the Nobles at Western Thebes, the two young men made such good use of their knowledge that Pharaoh soon realized that his treasure was beginning to grow mysteriously less.

Rameses was at a loss to understand how the thieves got in, for the royal seals were never broken, but get in they certainly did. Pharaoh was fast becoming a miser, and he paid frequent visits to his Treasure House and knew every object of value in it—and the treasure continued to go.

At last Pharaoh commanded that cunning traps and meshes should be set near the chests and vessels from which the treasure was disappearing.

This was done secretly; and when next the two brothers made their way into the Treasure House by the secret entrance to collect more gold and jewels, the first to step across the floor towards the chests was caught in one of the traps and knew at once that he could not escape.

—From *Tales of Ancient Egypt*
by Roger Lancelyn Green

stop reading ➝■

Help the student identify the important elements in this story by asking the following questions:

Instructor: Who was Horemheb?
Student: He was the Master Builder.

Instructor: After the doors to the treasure chamber were locked, what was put on them?
Student: Pharaoh's seal was placed on them.

Instructor: How did Horemheb trick the Pharaoh?
Student: He built a secret passage into the treasure chamber.

Instructor: The story says that Horemheb was "able to

add to the reward which Pharaoh gave to him." What do you think this means?

Child: *He was stealing from the treasure chamber.* (You may need to prompt the student for this answer.)

Instructor: After Horemheb died, who began to use the secret passage to steal treasure?
Student: *Horemheb's two sons began to steal the treasure.*

Instructor: What did Pharaoh do when he found that his treasure was disappearing?
Student: *He set traps near the treasure.*

Instructor: Did the traps work?
Student: *Yes, one of the brothers was caught.*

Ask the student to provide a three-sentence summary of the passage. It should resemble one of the following:

> "The Pharaoh asked his Master Builder to build him a treasure room. The Master Builder made a secret passage into the treasure room. He and his sons stole the treasure."

> "Horemheb, who was the Pharaoh's Master Builder, made a treasure room with a secret passage. He used the passage to steal treasure. He told his sons about the passage before he died, and they used it to steal even more."

> "The Master Builder built the Pharaoh a treasure room with a secret passage. He used the passage to steal treasure, and after he died his sons used it too. But the Pharaoh set traps and caught one of the sons."

If the student has trouble condensing the information in the passage, ask the following three questions:

What did Horemheb do?
What did this allow him and his sons to do?
What did the Pharaoh do about it?

Write the student's narration down as he watches.

DAY TWO: Dictation

Tell the student that, in these sentences, pharaoh should not be capitalized because it does not stand for a particular person. It was capitalized in the Day One passage because it named a particular pharaoh, Rameses III.

Repeat the selection twice and then ask the student to repeat it back to you before he writes. Indicate the period after the first sentence with your voice. Remind the student that "pharaoh" is spelled with the "a" *before* the "o."

> The king of Egypt was called the pharaoh. The pharaohs of Egypt built pyramids to protect their treasures and their graves.

DAY THREE: Narration and Dictation

Tell the student that the following passage comes from the Greek historian Herodotus, and gives *his* version of the story. Roger Lancelyn Green used this passage as a basis for his own story.

Allow the student to read independently. Tell him to ask you if he comes across a word he doesn't know. The student will probably not know what "depredations" are—ask him to guess from context before telling him that "depredation" is "the act of robbing or plundering."

●— begin reading ———————————————————

FROM *THE HISTORIES*

This is Herodotus' version of this same story about the Egyptian king Rameses.

He wanted to store his money in a safe place, so he built a stone chamber as an extension off one of the outside walls of his residence. The builder, however, came up with the following crafty scheme. He cleverly fitted one of the stones in such a way that it would easily be removable from its wall by two men or even one. Anyway, the chamber was finished and the king stored his money in it. Time passed. At the end of his life, the builder summoned his sons (there were two of them) and told them of the plan he had put into effect while building the king's treasure-chamber, so that they would be comfortable for the rest of their lives. He explained precisely to them how to remove the stone and described its position in the wall. He told them that if they remembered his instructions, they would be the stewards of the king's treasury.

He died, and his sons soon set to work. They went by night to the royal residence and found the stone in the building. It was easy for them to handle, and they carried off a lot of money. When the king happened to go into the chamber next, he was surprised to see that the caskets were missing some money, but the seals on the door were still intact and the chamber had been locked up, so he could not blame anyone. But the same thing happened the next couple of times he opened the door as well: his money was obviously dwindling all the time (for the thieves had not stopped their depredations). So the king had traps made, and set them around the caskets which held the money. The thieves came as usual and one of them sneaked into the chamber, but as soon as he approached a casket he was caught in the trap.

—From *The Histories*
by Herodotus
trans. Robin Waterfield

stop reading →■

Help the student identify the important elements in this story by asking the following questions:

> **Instructor:** In this passage, the treasure chamber isn't built into a pyramid. What building is it part of?
> **Student:** *It is part of the king's palace.*

> **Instructor:** What kind of door did the builder put into the wall?
> **Student:** *He put a stone in the wall that could be taken out.*

> **Instructor:** To whom did the builder tell his secret?
> **Student:** *He told it to his sons.*

> **Instructor:** Why could the king not blame anyone for the thefts? Two reasons were given.
> **Student:** *The seals on the door weren't broken, and the chamber was locked.*

> **Instructor:** What did the king do to protect his treasure?
> **Student:** *He put traps around the treasure.*

> **Instructor:** What happened to the thieves?
> **Student:** *One of them was caught in a trap.*

Ask the student to provide a three-sentence summary of the passage. It should resemble one of the following:

> "The builder built a treasure-room onto the king's palace, but he

left a loose stone in the wall so that he could steal treasure. He told his sons about the stone before he died. His sons also stole treasure, but one of them got caught in a trap."

"The king told his builder to make a treasure-room. The builder left a removable stone in the wall, so that he and his sons could steal the treasure. When the king realized that his treasure was disappearing, he set a trap and caught one of the thieves."

"The builder planned to make himself and his sons comfortable with the king's treasure. So he left a loose stone in the wall, so that they could always get into the treasure-room. But the king set traps around the money, and one of the builder's sons was caught."

If the student has trouble condensing the information in the passage, ask the following three questions:

What did the builder do to the treasure-room?
Who stole the money?
How did the king respond to the disappearing money?

Write the student's narration down, but do not allow him to watch. Then dictate one or two sentences (15 to 18 words) back to the student.

Day Four: Dictation

Repeat the selection twice and then ask the student to repeat it back to you before he writes. Indicate the period after the first sentence with your voice. Give the student the correct spelling of "Lancelyn." If necessary, remind him that initials are capitalized and followed by a period.

Roger Lancelyn Green retold the stories of the Egyptians. When he was younger, he studied at Oxford, where his tutor was C. S. Lewis.

WEEKS 12–19

Follow the same pattern as above:

Day One: Narration Exercise

Choose reading passages of around six paragraphs or 30 to 35 lines from the student's literature, science, or history texts. After the student reads the passage independently, ask the student comprehension questions before requiring a brief, two- or three-sentence summary. Write the student's narration down as he watches.

Day Two: Dictation

Dictate selections of 15 to 18 words (two sentences) that the student has not yet seen. Repeat the selection twice, indicating dialogue or unusual punctuation with your voice. Have the student repeat the selection back to you before writing. You may prompt the student one additional time, if necessary, but encourage him to think first.

Over these eight weeks, look for selections that include the following elements. Point them out to the student after he writes.

Proper nouns .... Week 12
Helping verbs... Week 13
Direct objects following action verbs................ Weeks 14–15
State of being verbs and linking verbs, predicate
nominatives, and predicate adjectives .... Weeks 16–18
Command sentences and understood "you"...... Week 19

If you cannot find sentences that contain these elements, alternate choosing dictation sentences from the student's books and making up your own dictation sentences with these elements included; this will help the student to practice proper form.

Day Three: Narration and Dictation

Follow the narration guidelines above. Write the student's narration down, but do not allow him to watch; use two sentences of the narration as the day's dictation exercise.

Day Four: Dictation

Follow the dictation guidelines above.

Year Three, Weeks 20–27

Although narration passages will remain at the same length, you will begin to encourage the student to summarize without first answering comprehension questions; this is the next step in the progression towards independent writing, since the student will have to identify central elements on his own. As before, the student should try to do this from memory, but can glance back at the passage if necessary to refresh his memory.

Dictation exercises lengthen slightly to 16 to 20 words (two longer or three shorter sentences), taken down after three repetitions; you will continue to use two narration sentences for dictation.

The pattern of Week 20 will serve as the model for Weeks 21 through 27.

WEEK 20

Day One: Narration Exercise

Give the student the following passage to read. Tell him ahead of time that he'll need to give a three-sentence summary, but that you won't be asking comprehension questions first. You may also want to remind the student that the "ough" in "bough" is pronounced "ow."

●— begin reading ——————————————

"The Garden of Live Flowers"

This passage is from the sequel to Alice in Wonderland. *Alice has gotten through the mirror in her sitting-room, and finds herself in a magical land behind it. As she walks along through this land, she finds herself walking through a flower-garden.*

"O Tiger-lily," said Alice, addressing herself to one that was waving gracefully about in the wind, "I *wish* you could talk!"

"We *can* talk," said the Tiger-lily, "when there's

anybody worth talking to."

Alice was so astonished that she could not speak for a minute: it quite seemed to take her breath away. At length, as the Tiger-lily only went on waving about, she spoke again, in a timid voice—almost in a whisper. "And can *all* the flowers talk?"

"As well as *you* can," said the Tiger-lily. "And a great deal louder."

"It isn't manners for us to begin, you know," said the Rose, "and I really was wondering when you'd speak! Said I to myself, 'Her face has got *some* sense in it, though it's not a clever one!' Still, you're the right colour, and that goes a long way."

"I don't care about the colour," the Tiger-lily remarked. "If only her petals curled up a little more, she'd be all right."

Alice didn't like being criticised, so she began asking questions. "Aren't you sometimes frightened at being planted out here, with nobody to take care of you?"

"There's the tree in the middle," said the Rose. "What else is it good for?"

"But what could it do, if any danger came?" Alice asked.

"It says 'Bough-wow!' cried a Daisy. "That's why its branches are called boughs!"

"Didn't you know *that?*" cried another Daisy, and here they all began shouting together, till the air seemed quite full of little shrill voices.

"Silence, every one of you!" cried the Tiger-lily, waving itself passionately from side to side, and trembling with excitement. "They know I can't get at them!" it panted, bending its quivering head towards Alice, "or they wouldn't dare to do it!"

"Never mind!" Alice said in a soothing tone, and stooping down to the daisies, who were just beginning again, she whispered, "If you don't hold your tongues, I'll pick you!"

There was silence in a moment, and several of the pink daisies turned white.

"That's right!" said the Tiger-lily. "The daisies are worst of all. When one speaks, they all begin together, and it's enough to make one wither to hear the way they go on!"

"How is it you can all talk so nicely?" Alice said, hoping to get it into a better temper by a compliment. "I've been in many gardens before, but none of the flowers could talk."

"Put your hand down, and feel the ground," said the Tiger-lily. "Then you'll know why."

Alice did so. "It's very hard," she said, "but I don't see

what that has to do with it."

"In most gardens," the Tiger-lily said, "they make the beds too soft—so that the flowers are always asleep."

This sounded a very good reason, and Alice was quite pleased to know it. "I never thought of that before!" she said.

—From *Alice Through the Looking-Glass*
by Lewis Carroll

stop reading ▬

You will now ask the student to summarize the passage. A detail-oriented summary is more appropriate to this descriptive passage than a summary telling what happens. Since this is the first time the student has summarized without having the help of comprehension questions, use a "directed narration starter": tell him, "Describe the garden in three sentences." His answer should resemble one of the following:

"In the garden, all the flowers can talk. The Tiger-lily is the leader of the flowers. The tree at the center of the garden keeps them safe by saying 'Bough-wow.'"

"The flowers in the garden can all talk. Alice finds out that this is because the ground is so hard that they stay awake. In most gardens, the ground is so soft that the flowers fall asleep."

"The Tiger-lily and the Rose both talk to Alice. The daisies talk too, but they all talk at once and make too much noise. The tree at the center of the garden keeps the flowers safe by 'barking.'"

"The garden has tiger-lilies, roses, and pink daisies in it. All of them can talk because the ground is so hard that it keeps them awake. In the middle of the garden, there is a tree that keeps the flowers safe."

If the student has trouble choosing important details, ask these three questions:

> What flowers are in the garden?
> What reason does the Tiger-lily give for the flowers' ability to talk?
> What is at the center of the garden?

Write the narration down as the student watches.

DAY TWO: Dictation

Tell the student that this selection comes from the same chapter. In the garden, Alice meets the Red Queen from her chess set, now grown to life size. The Red Queen is quite bossy.

Before reading the selection, remind the student of the proper form for direct quotations. The Red Queen's actual words should be surrounded by quotation marks. The ending punctuation for each of the Red Queen's sentences should go *inside* the closing quotation marks. The phrase "said the Red Queen" is part of the previous sentence, so "said" should not be capitalized. "And" is capitalized because it begins a new sentence. Also remind the student that "Red Queen" is used as a proper name, so both words should be capitalized.

Now tell the student that you will read the selection three times. Be sure to indicate questions and statements with your voice; also, use a different voice for the Red Queen's actual words and your normal voice for the phrase "said the Red Queen."

Ask the student to repeat the entire selection back to you before he writes.

> "Where do you come from?" said the Red Queen. "And where are you going? Look up, speak nicely, and don't twiddle your fingers all the time."

DAY THREE: Narration and Dictation

Allow the student to read the following passage independently.

●— **begin reading** ——————————————

"QUEEN ALICE"

This chapter is near the end of the book. Alice has found herself in the middle of a life-size chess game, and has unexpectedly been made a queen. The other two queens, the Red and White Queens, have invited her to a dinner party in her honor.

Alice glanced nervously along the table, as she walked up the large hall, and noticed that there were about fifty guests, of all kinds: some were animals, some birds, and there were even a few flowers among them. "I'm glad they've come without waiting to be asked," she thought. "I should never have known who were the right people to invite!"

There were three chairs at the head of the table; the Red and White Queens had already taken two of them, but the middle one was empty. Alice sat down in it, rather uncomfortable in the silence, and longing for someone to speak.

At last the Red Queen began. "You've missed the soup and fish," she said. "Put on the joint!" And the waiters set a leg of mutton before Alice, who looked at it rather anxiously, as she had never had to carve a joint before.

"You look a little shy; let me introduce you to that leg of mutton," said the Red Queen. "Alice—Mutton;

Mutton—Alice." The leg of mutton got up in the dish and made a little bow to Alice; and Alice returned the bow, not knowing whether to be frightened or amused.

"May I give you a slice?" she said, taking up the knife and fork, and looking from one Queen to the other.

"Certainly not," the Red Queen said, very decidedly. "It isn't etiquette to cut anyone you've been introduced to. Remove the joint!" And the waiters carried it off, and brought a large plum-pudding in its place.

"I won't be introduced to the pudding, please," Alice said rather hastily, "or we shall get no dinner at all. May I give you some?"

But the Red Queen looked sulky, and growled "Pudding—Alice; Alice—Pudding. Remove the pudding!" and the waiters took it away so quickly that Alice couldn't return its bow.

However, she didn't see why the Red Queen should be the only one to give orders, so, as an experiment, she called out "Waiter! Bring back the pudding!" and there it was again in a moment like a conjuring-trick. It was so large that she couldn't help feeling a LITTLE shy with it, as she had been with the mutton; however, she conquered her shyness by a great effort and cut a slice and handed it to the Red Queen.

"What impertinence!" said the Pudding. "I wonder

how you'd like it, if I were to cut a slice out of YOU, you creature!"

It spoke in a thick, suety sort of voice, and Alice hadn't a word to say in reply: she could only sit and look at it and gasp.

"Make a remark," said the Red Queen: "it's ridiculous to leave all the conversation to the pudding!"

—From *Alice Through the Looking Glass*
by Lewis Carroll

stop reading ━■

You will now ask the student to summarize the passage. This selection lends itself to a narrative, story-like retelling. To guide the student towards this type of summary, ask him, "In three sentences, what happened at the dinner party?" His answer should resemble one of the following:

"The Red Queen introduced Alice to the leg of mutton, so then the waiters carried it off. Then she introduced Alice to the plum pudding, but Alice cut a slice out of it anyway. When she did, the pudding spoke to her."

"At the dinner, the Red Queen kept introducing Alice to the food. Then the waiters carried it off, because it isn't polite to eat food that you've been introduced to. Finally Alice cut the pudding—but the pudding talked back to her."

"Alice was hungry, but she couldn't eat her meat because she had been introduced to it. The Red Queen also introduced her to the pudding, but she decided to eat it anyway. When she cut a slice, it said, 'How would you like me to cut a slice out of you?'"

If the student has difficulty with this summary, ask the following three questions to help focus his thoughts:

Why couldn't Alice eat her leg of mutton?
What did she do to the pudding?
What did the pudding do in response?

Write the narration down, but do not allow the student to watch. Then dictate two or three sentences (around 16 to 20 words) back to the student.

DAY FOUR: Dictation

Tell the student that this selection comes from the chapter where Alice meets the two strange brothers, Tweedledum and Tweedledee. Spell those names for the student. Then warn him that this selection is one very long sentence with seven commas in it. Make sure to indicate the commas by pausing significantly when you reach each one.

Read the sentence three times and then ask the student to repeat it back to you. You may need to repeat it additional times before he is able to do this. Don't be afraid to prompt him again as he writes; this is a difficult selection.

> So she wandered on, talking to herself as she went, till, on turning a sharp corner, she came upon two fat little men, so suddenly that she could not help starting back, but in another moment she recovered herself, feeling sure that they must be Tweedledum and Tweedledee.

WEEKS 21–27

Follow the same pattern as above:

DAY ONE: Narration Exercise

Choose reading passages of around six paragraphs or 30 to 35 lines from the student's literature, science, or history texts. After the student reads the passage independently, ask him either to describe the scene, or to give you a brief narrative summary of the passage's events. Write the student's narration down as he watches.

DAY TWO: Dictation

Dictate selections of 16 to 20 words (two longer or three shorter sentences) that the student has not yet seen. Repeat the selection two or three times depending on difficulty, indicating dialogue or unusual punctuation with your voice. Have the student repeat the selection back to you before writing. You may prompt the student one additional time, if necessary, but encourage him to think first.

Over these seven weeks, look for selections that include the following elements. Point them out to the student after he writes.

If you cannot find sentences that contain these elements, alternate choosing dictation sentences from the student's books and making up your own dictation sentences with these elements included; this will help the student to practice proper form.

DAY THREE: Narration and Dictation

Follow the narration guidelines above. Write the student's narration down, but do not allow him to watch; use two or three sentences of the narration (around 16 to 20 words) as the day's dictation exercise.

DAY FOUR: Dictation

Follow the dictation guidelines above.

Year Three, Weeks 28–35

Narration exercises will lengthen slightly to seven to eight paragraphs, roughly 35 to 45 lines; the student will continue to read the passage independently and will then answer directed narration questions without first answering comprehension questions. As before, the student should try to do this from memory, but can refer back to the passage if necessary.

Dictation exercises will remain at 16 to 20 words, two longer or three shorter sentences, taken down after three repetitions.

Rather than dictating narration sentences to the student, you will now help her repeat one sentence of her narration exercise out loud, to herself, so that she can take the sentence down from her own dictation. This is the final step before the student begins to write independently.

The pattern of Week 28 will serve as the model for Weeks 29 through 35.

WEEK 28

DAY ONE: Narration Exercise

Give the student the following passage to read. Tell her ahead of time that she'll need to give a three-sentence summary of what happens, but that you won't be asking comprehension questions first.

— begin reading —————————————————————————

"MARILLA CUTHBERT IS SURPRISED"

Marilla and Matthew Cuthbert are an elderly brother and sister who live together on Prince Edward Island, in Canada. They decide that they need help on their farm, so they send away to an orphanage in a nearby town, asking for a boy who can come live with them. Matthew Cuthbert goes to pickup the orphan at the train station—but when he gets there, he finds that they've sent a little girl instead. He doesn't know what to do, so he takes the little girl home.

Marilla came briskly forward as Matthew opened the door. But when her eyes fell on the odd little figure in the stiff, ugly dress, with the long braids of red hair and the eager, luminous eyes, she stopped short in amazement.

"Matthew Cuthbert, who's that?" she ejaculated. "Where is the boy?"

"There wasn't any boy," said Matthew wretchedly. "There was only HER."

He nodded at the child, remembering that he had never even asked her name.

"No boy! But there MUST have been a boy," insisted Marilla. "We sent word to Mrs. Spencer to bring a boy."

"Well, she didn't. She brought HER. I asked the station-master. And I had to bring her home. She couldn't be left there, no matter where the mistake had come in."

"Well, this is a pretty piece of business!" ejaculated Marilla.

During this dialogue the child had remained silent, her eyes roving from one to the other, all the animation fading out of her face. Suddenly she seemed to grasp the full meaning of what had been said. Dropping her precious carpet-bag she sprang forward a step and clasped her hands.

"You don't want me!" she cried. "You don't want me because I'm not a boy! I might have expected it. Nobody ever did want me. I might have known it was all too beautiful to last. I might have known nobody really did want me. Oh, what shall I do? I'm going to burst into tears!"

Burst into tears she did. Sitting down on a chair by the table, flinging her arms out upon it, and burying her face in them, she proceeded to cry stormily. Marilla and Matthew looked at each other deprecatingly across the stove. Neither of them knew what to say or do. Finally Marilla stepped lamely into the breach.

"Well, well, there's no need to cry so about it."

"Yes, there IS need!" The child raised her head quickly, revealing a tear-stained face and trembling lips. "YOU would cry, too, if you were an orphan and had come to a place you thought was going to be home and found that they didn't want you because you weren't a boy. Oh, this is the most TRAGICAL thing that ever happened to me!"

Something like a reluctant smile, rather rusty from long disuse, mellowed Marilla's grim expression.

"Well, don't cry any more. We're not going to turn you out-of-doors to-night. You'll have to stay here until we investigate this affair. What's your name?"

The child hesitated for a moment.

"Will you please call me Cordelia?" she said eagerly.

"CALL you Cordelia? Is that your name?"

"No-o-o, it's not exactly my name, but I would love to be called Cordelia. It's such a perfectly elegant name."

"I don't know what on earth you mean. If Cordelia isn't your name, what is?"

"Anne Shirley," reluctantly faltered forth the owner of that name, "but, oh, please do call me Cordelia. It can't matter much to you what you call me if I'm only going to be here a little while, can it? And Anne is such an unromantic name."

"Unromantic fiddlesticks!" said the unsympathetic Marilla. "Anne is a real good plain sensible name. You've no need to be ashamed of it."

—From *Anne of Green Gables*
by Lucy Maud Montgomery

stop reading ─■

You will now ask the student to summarize the passage. This selection lends itself to a narrative, story-like retelling. To guide the student towards this type of summary, ask her, "In three sentences, what happened when Marilla and Anne met each other?" Her answer should resemble one of the following:

> "Marilla was surprised to see that Matthew had brought home a girl. The little girl realized that she wasn't wanted, and burst into tears. Marilla told her not to cry, and asked her what her name was."

> "When Matthew and Anne came into the house, Marilla asked where the boy was. Anne began to cry because no one wanted her, and Marilla asked what her name was. Anne asked Marilla

to call her Cordelia, but Marilla said that Anne was a good plain name."

"Matthew told Marilla that he had to bring Anne home even though she was a girl. Anne realized that she wasn't supposed to be there, and began to cry. But Marilla told her that she could stay while they found out what the mistake was."

If the student has difficulty with this summary, ask the following three questions to help focus her thoughts:

What was Marilla's reaction when she saw Anne?
What did Anne do when she realized that there had been a mistake?
When Anne began to cry, how did Marilla respond?

Write the narration down as the student watches.

DAY TWO: Dictation

Tell the student that this selection is from Chapter One of *Anne of Green Gables*, "Mrs. Rachel Lynde Is Surprised." Mrs. Rachel Lynde, the Cuthbert's nosy neighbor, has just found out that Marilla and Matthew have sent to the orphanage for a boy.

Be sure to tell the student that there are two exclamation points in the selection; indicate them with your voice while you read. You may also want to point out that the last two sentences are fragments; this is an appropriate use of a fragment in writing.

> **Mrs. Rachel felt that she had received a severe mental jolt. She thought in exclamation points. A boy! Marilla and Matthew Cuthbert of all people adopting a boy!**

DAY THREE: Narration and Dictation

This passage is shorter than the previous passage because it is so full of detail. Give the selection to the student to read independently. Tell her that while she certainly doesn't have to remember every detail, you will be asking her to describe Prince Edward Island in her summary.

●— **begin reading** —————————————————————————

"CARTIER COMES TO PRINCE EDWARD ISLAND"

This is from Pioneers in Canada, *a classic text about Canadian history written by Harry Johnston almost a hundred years ago. Johnston describes the journey that the French explorer Jacques Cartier made to the coast of North America in 1534. On this journey, Cartier came to Prince Edward Island, where* Anne of Green Gables *is set.*

Before you read, you should know that guillemots are birds related to the now-extinct great auk. Both guillemots and great auks looked a little bit like penguins. Gannets are seabirds that look something like seagulls, and eider ducks are sea ducks that live in cold areas. "Eiderdown," a kind of duck feather used to stuff mattresses, is named after the eider duck.

As he sailed northwards, past the deeply indented fiords and bays of eastern Newfoundland (the shores of which were still hugged by the winter ice), he and his men were much impressed with the incredible numbers of the sea fowl settled for nesting purposes on the rocky islands, especially on Funk Island. These birds were guillemots, puffins, great auks, gannets (called by Cartier *margaulx*), and probably gulls and eider duck. To his sailors—always hungry and partly fed on salted provisions, as seamen were down to a few years ago—this inexhaustible supply of fresh food was a source of great enjoyment. They were indifferent, no doubt, to the fishy flavour of the auks and the guillemots, and only noticed that they were splendidly fat. Moreover, the birds attracted polar bears "as large as cows and as white as swans." The bears would swim off from the shore to the islands (unless they could reach them by crossing the ice), and the sailors occasionally killed the bears and ate their flesh, which they compared in excellence and taste to veal.

Passing through the Straits of Belle Isle, Cartier's ships entered the Gulf of St. Lawrence. They had previously visited the adjoining coast of Labrador, and there had encountered their first natives, members of some Algonquin tribe from Canada, who had come north for seal fishing (Cartier is clever enough to notice and describe their birch-bark canoes). After examining the west coast of Newfoundland, Cartier's ships sailed on past the Magdalen Islands (stopping every now and then off some islet to collect supplies of sea birds, for the rocky ground was covered with them as thickly as a meadow with grass). On the shores of these islands they noticed "several great beasts like oxen, which have two tusks in the mouth similar to those of the elephant." These were walruses.

He reached the north coast of Prince Edward Island, and this lovely country received from him an enthusiastic description. The pine trees, the junipers, yews, elms, poplars, ash, and willows, the beeches and the maples, made the forest not only full of delicious and stimulating odours, but lovely in its varied tints of green. In the natural meadows and forest clearings there were red and white currants, gooseberries, strawberries, raspberries, a vetch which produced edible peas, and a grass with a grain like rye. The forest abounded in pigeons, and the climate was pleasant and warm.

—From *Pioneers in Canada*
by Sir Harry Johnston

stop reading —■

You will now ask the student to summarize the passage. To guide her towards a detail-oriented summary, simply say, "Describe Prince Edward Island in two or three sentences. Be sure to use specific names for trees, plants, and animals." Her answer should resemble one of the following:

"Prince Edward Island has pines, willows, maples, and many other trees. The island also has strawberries, raspberries, and grain. There are many pigeons in the forests."

"The forests on Prince Edward Island are many different colors of green because there are so many different trees—like pines, elms, and beeches. The island is pleasant and warm, and there are gooseberries, strawberries, peas, and raspberries growing there."

"Jacques Cartier sailed to the north end of Prince Edward Island and described it. He said that there were many different trees, such as pines and maples, and wild berries, like strawberries and raspberries."

If the student has trouble choosing important details, ask these three questions:

Name three trees that were in the forests.
Name three foods that grew in the meadows and forests.
Can you remember one more thing about the island?

(If the student draws a blank, ask her what the weather was like, whether there were any birds, or which explorer landed on it.)

Write the narration down, but do not allow the student to watch. Then ask her whether she can repeat the first sentence of the narration to herself. If not, read her the first sentence of the narration ONLY. Tell her to listen carefully, since you will only read it once. Encourage her to repeat it to herself until she can remember it, and then to say it out loud to herself as she writes it down.

DAY FOUR: Dictation

Tell the student that although Prince Edward Island is cold in the winter, Jacques Cartier landed on the island in midsummer. Anne also arrived at the Cuthbert farm in summer; this selection from Chapter Four, "Morning at Green Gables," describes when she first looked out of her window.

Be sure to indicate the period by pausing, and use a questioning voice for the two questions at the end.

> Anne dropped on her knees and gazed out into
> the June morning, her eyes glistening with delight.
> Oh, wasn't it beautiful? Wasn't it a lovely place?

WEEKS 29–35

Follow the same pattern as above.

DAY ONE: Narration Exercise

Choose reading passages of seven to eight paragraphs (around 35 to 45 lines) from the student's literature, science, or history texts. After the student reads the passage independently, ask her either to describe the scene, or to give you a brief narrative summary of the passage's events. Write the student's narration down as she watches.

DAY TWO: Dictation

Dictate selections of 16 to 20 words (two longer or three shorter sentences) that the student has not yet seen. Repeat the selection three times depending on difficulty, indicating dialogue or unusual punctuation with your voice. Have the student repeat the selection back to you before writing.

Over these seven weeks, look for selections that include the following elements. Point them out to the student after she writes.

Commas in direct address............................ Week 29
Contractions (won't, don't, didn't, I'll, you'll).... Weeks 30–31
Direct quotations at beginning, middle, and
end of sentences .... Weeks 32–33
Comparative and superlative adjectives .... Week 34
Interjections .... Week 35

If you cannot find sentences that contain these elements, alternate choosing dictation sentences from the student's books and making up your own dictation sentences with these elements included; this will help the student to practice proper form.

DAY THREE: Narration and Dictation

Follow the narration guidelines above. Write the narration down, but do not allow the student to watch. Then ask her whether she can repeat the first sentence of the narration to herself. If not, read her the first sentence of the narration ONLY. Tell her to listen carefully, since you will only read it once. Encourage her to repeat it to herself until she can remember it, and then to say it out loud to herself as she writes it down.

DAY FOUR: Dictation

Follow the dictation guidelines above.

Year Three Mastery Evaluation, Week 36

By this point, the student should be able to read a passage independently, sum it up in two or three sentences, write down the first sentence of her own narration, and take dictation exercises of around 20 words after three repetitions.

If the student struggles with this week's assignments, plan on spending a few more weeks practicing her "trouble spots" before moving on.

NARRATION EVALUATION

Give the following passage to the student to read independently

● — begin reading ———————————————————————

This book was first published in 1944. It is the story of the animals who live on a deserted farm called the Hill. One of these animals is Little Georgie, a young rabbit who lives with his family beneath the Hill. In this excerpt, Little Georgie is hopping past a neighbor's house, not really paying attention, when the neighbor's dog, the Old Hound, surprises him and begins to chase him.

You should know that "Porkey" is the name of Georgie's friend the woodchuck, an animal also called a "groundhog" in some parts of the country.

Instinctively Little Georgie made several wide springs that carried him temporarily out of harm's way. He paused a fraction of a second to tighten the knapsack strap and then set off at a good steady pace. "Don't waste speed on a plodder" was Father's rule. He tried a few checks and doubles and circlings, although he knew they were pretty useless. The great fields were too bare, and the Old Hound knew all the tricks. No matter how he turned and dodged, the Old Hound was always there, coming along at his heavy gallop. He looked for Woodchuck burrows, but there were none in sight. "Well, I guess I'll have to run it out," said Little Georgie.

He pulled the knapsack strap tighter, laced back his ears, put his stomach to the ground, and RAN. And *how* he ran!

The warm sun had loosened his muscles; the air was invigorating; Little Georgie's leaps grew longer and longer. Never had he felt so young and strong. His legs were like coiled springs of steel that released themselves of their own accord. He was hardly conscious of any effort, only of his hind feet pounding the ground, and each time they hit, those wonderful springs released and shot him through the air. He sailed over fences and stone walls as though they were mole runs. Why, this was almost like flying! Now he understood what Zip the Swallow had been driving at when he tried to describe what it was like. He glanced back at the Old Hound, far behind now, but still coming along at his plodding gallop. He was old and must be tiring, while he, Little Georgie, felt stronger and more vigorous at every leap. Why didn't the old fool give up and go home?

And then, as he shot over the brow of a slight rise, he suddenly knew. *He had forgotten Deadman's Brook!* There it lay before him, broad and deep, curving out in a great silvery loop. He, the son of Father, gentleman hunter from the Bluegrass, had been driven into a trap, a trap that even Porkey should have been able to avoid! Whether he turned to right or left the loop of the creek hemmed him in and the Old Hound could easily cut him off. There was nothing for it but to jump!

This sickening realization had not reduced his speed; now he redoubled it. The slope helped, and his soaring leaps became prodigious. The wind whistled through his laced-back ears. Still he kept his head, as Father would have wished him to. He picked a spot where the bank was high and firm; he spaced his jumps so they would come out exactly right.

The take-off was perfect. He put every ounce of leg muscle into that final kick and sailed out into space. Below him he could see the cream-puff clouds mirrored in the dark water, he could see the pebbles on the bottom and the silver flash of frightened minnows dashing away from his flying shadow. Then, with a breath-taking thump, he landed, turned seven somersaults, and came up sitting in a clump of soft lush grass.

He froze, motionless except for heaving sides, and watched the Old Hound come thundering down the slope, slide to a stop and, after eyeing the water

disgustedly, take his way slowly homeward, his dripping
tongue almost dragging the ground.

—From *Rabbit Hill*
by Robert Lawson

stop reading ——■

Now ask the student to summarize the passage in three sentences. His
answer should resemble one of the following:

> "Little Georgie ran away from the Old Hound, so fast that it felt
> like flying. But when he came over a hill, he saw Deadman's
> Brook in front of him. He leaped all the way over the brook, and
> the Old Hound gave up and went slowly home."

> "The Old Hound was chasing Little Georgie, and Little Georgie
> could not find anywhere to hide. He wondered why the Old
> Hound didn't give up, until he came to Deadman's Brook. He
> had to jump over it, even though he was frightened."

> "Little George was running away from the Old Hound when he
> saw a stream in front of him. It was so wide that he didn't think
> he could jump across it. But he leaped as hard as he could, sailed
> across, and landed safely on the other side."

Write the narration down, but do not allow the student to watch. Then
read him the first sentence of the narration ONLY ONCE. Tell the student
to repeat the sentence to himself, and then to say it out loud to himself as he
writes it down.

Dictation Evaluation

Tell the student that, before Georgie sets off on his journey, his father
wants to make sure that he knows how to cross over a bridge safely. He asks
Georgie, "What do you do when you come to a bridge?" This is Georgie's
response (from *Rabbit Hill*, p. 37):

> "I hide well," answered Georgie, "and wait a good

long time. I look all around for dogs. I look up the road for cars and down the road for cars."

Year Four

Fourth Grade (or Level Four, for Older Writers)

Year Four leads the student through the final task of elementary writing: creating sentences in the mind and then putting them down on paper. The student continues to develop his memory by practicing increasingly complex dictation exercises, eventually writing brief paragraphs from dictation; this skill helps him hold his own words in mind as he writes. He also practices recognizing the central elements in longer and more difficult reading selections. By the end of Year Four, the student will be able to read a 12-paragraph selection, summarize it in his own words, and write the summary down without assistance. With the basic skills of writing mastered, he will be prepared to begin original writing.

The lessons that follow spell out an entire week's assignments whenever the student progresses from one step to the next. If you wish, you can then follow the pattern of this model work, but choose your own copywork and narration assignments. Alternatively, you can use the Year Four workbook; this provides a full sequence of copywork and narration assignments that introduce the student sequentially to the necessary grammatical elements.

Year Four, Weeks 1–10

Narration exercises lengthen to eight to ten paragraphs, or roughly 40 to 50 lines. After reading the passage independently, the student will answer a directed narration question with a three- or four-sentence narration. You will then ask the student to repeat the first narration sentence back to himself, listen to himself, and write the sentence down.

Other dictation exercises should be roughly 20 words (two longer or three shorter sentences), taken down after three repetitions.

The pattern of Week 1 will be followed in Weeks 2 through 10.

WEEK 1

DAY ONE: Narration and Dictation

Allow the student to read the following story independently.

● — **begin reading** ———————————————————

"THE EMPEROR'S NEW CLOTHES"

*This is a tale by Hans Christian Andersen, the Danish fairy-tale writer who lived 1805–1875. You probably know this story already, but pay close attention; you will need to remember **only** the details found in this particular version of the tale.*

Many years ago, there was an Emperor, who was so excessively fond of new clothes, that he spent all his money in dress. He had a different suit for each hour of the day; and as of any other king or emperor, one is accustomed to say, "he is sitting in council," it was always said of him, "The Emperor is sitting in his wardrobe."

One day, two rogues, calling themselves weavers,

made their appearance. They gave out that they knew how to weave stuffs of the most beautiful colors and elaborate patterns, the clothes manufactured from which should have the wonderful property of remaining invisible to everyone who was unfit for the office he held, or who was extraordinarily simple in character.

"These must, indeed, be splendid clothes!" thought the Emperor. "Had I such a suit, I might at once find out what men in my realms are unfit for their office, and also be able to distinguish the wise from the foolish! This stuff must be woven for me immediately." And he caused large sums of money to be given to both the weavers in order that they might begin their work directly.

So the two pretended weavers set up two looms, and affected to work very busily, though in reality they did nothing at all. They asked for the most delicate silk and the purest gold thread; put both into their own knapsacks; and then continued their pretended work at the empty looms until late at night.

The whole city was talking of the splendid cloth which the Emperor had ordered to be woven at his own expense. And now the Emperor himself wished to see the costly manufacture, while it was still in the loom. Accompanied by a select number of officers of the court, he went to the crafty impostors, who, as soon as they were aware of the Emperor's approach, went on working more diligently than ever; although they still did not pass a single thread through the looms.

"How is this?" said the Emperor to himself. "I can see nothing! This is indeed a terrible affair! Am I a simpleton, or am I unfit to be an Emperor? That would be the worst thing that could happen—Oh! the cloth is charming," said he, aloud. And he smiled most graciously, and looked closely at the empty looms; for on no account would he say that he could not see. All his retinue now strained their eyes, hoping to discover something on the looms, but they could see no more than the others; nevertheless, they all exclaimed, "Oh, how beautiful!" and advised his majesty to have some new clothes made from this splendid material, for the approaching procession.

The rogues sat up the whole of the night before the day on which the procession was to take place, and had sixteen lights burning, so that everyone might see how anxious they were to finish the Emperor's new suit. They pretended to roll the cloth off the looms; cut the air with their scissors; and sewed with needles without any thread in them. "See!" cried they, at last. "The Emperor's new clothes are ready!"

And now the Emperor, with all the grandees of his court, came to the weavers; and the rogues raised their arms, as if in the act of holding something up, saying, "Here are your Majesty's trousers! Here is the scarf! Here is the mantle! The whole suit is as light as a cobweb; one might fancy one has nothing at all on, when dressed in it; that, however, is the great virtue of this delicate cloth."

"Yes indeed!" said all the courtiers, although not one of them could see anything of this exquisite manufacture.

"If your Imperial Majesty will be graciously pleased to take off your clothes, we will fit on the new suit, in front of the looking glass."

The Emperor was accordingly undressed, and the rogues pretended to array him in his new suit; the Emperor turning round, from side to side, before the looking glass. The lords of the bedchamber, who were to carry his Majesty's train felt about on the ground, as if they were lifting up the ends of the mantle; and pretended to be carrying something; for they would by no means betray anything like simplicity, or unfitness for their office.

So now the Emperor walked under his high canopy in the midst of the procession, through the streets of his capital; and all the people standing by, and those at the windows, cried out, "Oh! How beautiful are our Emperor's new clothes! What a magnificent train there is to the mantle; and how gracefully the scarf hangs!" in short, no one would allow that he could not see these much-admired clothes; because, in doing so, he would have declared himself either a simpleton or unfit for his office.

"But the Emperor has nothing at all on!" said a little child.

"Listen to the voice of innocence!" exclaimed his father; and what the child had said was whispered from one to another.

"But he has nothing at all on!" at last cried out all the people. The Emperor was vexed, for he knew that the people were right; but he thought the procession must go on now!

—Condensed slightly from *Andersen's Fairy Tales*
by Hans Christian Andersen

_____ **stop reading** →∎

You will now ask the student to summarize the passage in three or four sentences. To guide him towards a brief summary, say, "Tell me what happened to the Emperor in the story" (this will help to keep him from getting bogged down in descriptions of the thieves). His answer should resemble one of the following:

> "The Emperor ordered new, splendid clothes from two men who offered to make him magical clothing. When the weavers showed him the new clothes, he could not see them—but he didn't want to admit it, so he pretended to put them on. Everyone else pretended to see them too, until a child said, 'The Emperor has nothing on!'"

"An Emperor who loved clothes ordered magic robes from two thieves. They told him that the clothes would be invisible to anyone who was stupid or unworthy. When the Emperor went to see the new clothes, he saw nothing at all—but he was embarrassed to say so. He pretended to put them and marched out in front of his people with no clothes on."

"The Emperor bought magic clothes that would be invisible to anyone who was simple or unfit. The tricksters who promised to make the clothes took his money, and then showed him empty looms. But the Emperor was ashamed to say that he couldn't see anything, so he pretended to admire the clothes. He even pretended to put them on—and almost everyone else pretended to see them too."

If the student has trouble choosing important details, ask these three questions:

> What did the Emperor think he was buying?
> What did he actually get?
> Why didn't he admit that he was being robbed?

Write the narration down, but do not allow the student to watch. Then ask him whether he can repeat the first sentence of the narration to himself. If not, read him the first sentence of the narration ONLY. Tell him to listen carefully, since you will only read it once. Encourage him to repeat it to himself until he can remember it, and then to say it out loud to himself as he writes it down.

DAY TWO: Dictation

Tell the student that the following selection, also from "The Emperor's New Clothes," is all one long sentence, with three commas in it. Make sure to pause at each comma. Give any spelling help needed.

Tell the student that you will read the selection three times. If necessary, you can prompt him a fourth time, but ask him to think hard first and try to "hear" the sentence in his head. He can say the sentence out loud if he finds this helpful.

> The impostors requested him very courteously to be so good as to come nearer their looms, and then asked him whether the design pleased him, and whether the colors were not very beautiful, while at the same time pointing to the empty frames.

DAY THREE: Narration and Dictation

Allow the student to read the following story independently.

●— **begin reading** ————————————————————

THE LEAPFROG

This is another of Hans Christian Andersen's fairy tales. This story is more difficult than the story of the Emperor's New Clothes, so you may want to read it more than once before you try to summarize it.

A Flea, a Grasshopper, and a Leapfrog once wanted to see which could jump highest; and they invited the whole world, and everybody else besides who chose to come to see the festival. Three famous jumpers were they, as everyone would say, when they all met together in the room.

"I will give my daughter to him who jumps highest," exclaimed the King; "for it is not so amusing where there is no prize to jump for."

The Flea was the first to step forward. He had exquisite manners, and bowed to the company on all sides; for he had noble blood, and was, moreover, accustomed to the society of man alone; and that makes a great difference.

Then came the Grasshopper. He was considerably heavier, but he was well-mannered, and wore a green uniform, which he had by right of birth; he said, moreover, that he belonged to a very ancient Egyptian family, and that in the house where he then was, he was thought much of. The fact was, he had been just brought out of the fields, and put in a pasteboard house, three stories high, all made of cards with the colored side inwards; and doors and windows cut out of the body of the Queen of Hearts. "I sing so well," said he, "that sixteen native grasshoppers who have chirped from infancy, and yet got no house built of cards to live in, grew thinner than they were before for sheer vexation when they heard me."

It was thus that the Flea and the Grasshopper gave an account of themselves, and thought they were quite good enough to marry a Princess.

The Leapfrog said nothing; but people gave it as their opinion, that he therefore thought the more; and when the housedog snuffed at him with his nose, he confessed the Leapfrog was of good family. The old councilor, who had had three orders given him to make him hold his tongue, asserted that the Leapfrog was a prophet; for that one could see on his back, if there would be a severe or mild winter, and that was what one could not see even on the back of the man who writes the almanac.

"I say nothing, it is true," exclaimed the King; "but I have my own opinion, notwithstanding."

Now the trial was to take place. The Flea jumped so high that nobody could see where he went to; so they all asserted he had not jumped at all; and that was dishonorable.

The Grasshopper jumped only half as high; but he leaped into the King's face, who said that was ill-mannered.

The Leapfrog stood still for a long time lost in thought; it was believed at last he would not jump at all.

"I only hope he is not unwell," said the housedog; when, pop! he made a jump all on one side into the lap of the Princess, who was sitting on a little golden stool close by.

Hereupon the King said, "There is nothing above my daughter; therefore to bound up to her is the highest jump that can be made; but for this, one must possess understanding, and the Leapfrog has shown that he has understanding. He is brave and intellectual."

And so he won the Princess.

"It's all the same to me," said the Flea. "She may have the old Leapfrog, for all I care. I jumped the highest; but in this world merit seldom meets its reward. A fine exterior is what people look at now-a-days." The Flea then went into foreign service, where, it is said, he was killed.

The Grasshopper sat without on a green bank, and reflected on worldly things; and he said too, "Yes, a fine exterior is everything—a fine exterior is what people care about." And then he began chirping his peculiar melancholy song, from which we have taken this history; and which may, very possibly, be all untrue, although it does stand here printed in black and white.

—Condensed slightly from *Andersen's Fairy Tales*
by Hans Christian Andersen

stop reading ⟶■

You will now ask the student to summarize the passage. To guide him towards a succinct summary, say, "Tell me what happened to each of the characters in the story." There are various correct responses to this prompt, but his answer should resemble one of the following:

> "A flea, a grasshopper, and a leapfrog had a jumping contest. The flea jumped so high that no one could see him. The grasshopper jumped into the king's face. But the leapfrog jumped into the princess's lap. He won the contest, because the princess was the highest in the land."

> "A flea, a grasshopper, and a leapfrog had a jumping contest. Whoever jumped highest would win the princess. The flea jumped so high that no one saw him and the grasshopper jumped into the king's face. But the leapfrog jumped into the princess's

lap and won."

"A flea, a grasshopper, and a leapfrog had a jumping contest to see who could jump highest. The leapfrog won, because he jumped into the princess's lap. So the leapfrog won the princess, the flea went to a foreign land and was killed, and the grasshopper sat on a bank and sang."

If the student has trouble choosing important details, ask these three questions:

Who were the three characters, and what were they doing?
Which character won?
Why did he win?

This prompt will steer him towards a summary that resembles the first and second answers. Alternatively, you can ask:

Who won the contest?
Why did he win?
What happened to the flea and the grasshopper afterwards?

Write the narration down, but do not allow the student to watch. Then ask him whether he can repeat the first sentence of the narration to himself. If not, read him the first sentence of the narration ONLY. Tell him to listen carefully, since you will only read it once. Encourage him to repeat it to himself until he can remember it, and then to say it out loud to himself as he writes it down.

DAY FOUR: Dictation

Tell the student that there are two sentences in the following dictation exercise. One of the sentences has a semicolon in the middle. Remind the student that a semicolon links two independent sentences without a coordinating conjunction. When you dictate the sentences, be sure to make a long pause at the period, and a much shorter pause at the semicolon.

Tell the student that International Children's Book Day is the name of a particular holiday, which means that all four words should be capitalized.

Tell the student that you will read the selection three times. If necessary, you can prompt him a fourth time, but ask him to think hard first and try to "hear" the sentence in his head. He can say the sentence out loud if he finds this helpful.

> Hans Christian Andersen was born in Denmark on April 2, 1805. Today, his birthday is an international holiday celebrating reading; it is called International Children's Book Day.

WEEKS 2–10

DAY ONE: Narration and Dictation

Choose reading passages of eight to ten paragraphs (roughly 40 to 45 lines) from the student's literature, science, or history texts. After the student reads the passage independently, ask him either to describe the scene, or to give you a brief narrative summary of the passage's events. Write the narration down, but do not allow the student to watch. Then ask him whether he can repeat the first sentence of the narration to himself. If not, read him the first sentence of the narration ONLY. Tell him to listen carefully, since you will only read it once. Encourage him to repeat it to himself until he can remember it, and then to say it out loud to himself as he writes it down.

DAY TWO: Dictation

Dictate selections of roughly 20 words (two longer or three shorter sentences) that the student has not yet seen. Tell the student that you will read the selection three times. If necessary, you can prompt him a fourth time, but ask him to think hard first and try to "hear" the sentence in his head. He can say the sentence out loud if he finds this helpful.

Be sure to indicate any dialogue or unusual punctuation with your voice. If there are any unusual elements in the selection, tell the student to watch out for them.

Over these nine weeks, look for selections that include the following elements. Point them out to the student after he writes.

Irregular plural nouns .... Week 2

Plurals of nouns that end in s, sh, ch, x, z, y .... Week 3

Collective nouns (i.e., class, nation, mob, family) .... Week 4

Proper names of people, places, and holidays ... Week 5

Proper format for titles of books (capitalize and underline or italicize) and poems, short stories, and songs (capitalize and enclose in quotation marks) .... Weeks 6–7

Demonstratives (this, that, these, those, etc.) used both as pronouns and as adjectives .... Weeks 8–9

Fragments and complete sentences .... Week 10

If you cannot find sentences that contain these elements, alternate choosing dictation sentences from the student's books and making up your own dictation sentences with these elements included; this will help the student to practice proper form.

Day Three: Narration and Dictation

Follow the narration and dictation guidelines above.

Day Four: Dictation

Follow the dictation guidelines above.

Year Four, Weeks 11–19

Narration exercises will remain at eight to ten paragraphs, and you will continue to ask the student directed narration questions to point him towards the appropriate kind of summary. However, you will begin to ask the student to repeat to himself and write down the first *two* sentences of his own narration.

Dictation exercises will remain at around 20 words, but will take the form of paragraphs; you will introduce the student to the form of a paragraph and explain that a paragraph is organized around a single idea.

The pattern of Week 11 will be followed in Weeks 12 through 19.

WEEK 11

DAY ONE: Narration and Dictation

Allow the student to read the following story independently.

● — begin reading ——————————————————————

"PLAYING PILGRIMS"

This is the opening scene in Little Women, *by Louisa May Alcott. Louisa May Alcott lived during the American Civil War; she worked as a nurse in an army hospital, caring for wounded soldiers.*

Little Women *is about the March family—four girls named Meg, Jo, Beth, and Amy, their mother, and their father. Mr. March is away, fighting in the Civil War on the side of the North. In this passage, Mrs. March has just received a telegram saying that her husband has been wounded and that she should travel to the hospital in Washington, D.C., immediately. This is a long journey for Mrs. March, who doesn't have much money, and she starts to get ready to leave at once.*

You will need to know that, in those days, women could

earn money by selling their hair to barbers, who made the hair into wigs for other customers.

The short afternoon wore away. All other errands were done, and Meg and her mother busy at some necessary needlework, while Beth and Amy got tea, and Hannah finished her ironing with what she called a "slap and a bang", but still Jo did not come. They began to get anxious, and Laurie went off to find her, for no one knew what freak Jo might take into her head. He missed her, however, and she came walking in with a very queer expression of countenance, for there was a mixture of fun and fear, satisfaction and regret in it, which puzzled the family as much as did the roll of bills she laid before her mother, saying with a little choke in her voice, "That's my contribution toward making Father comfortable and bringing him home!"

"My dear, where did you get it? Twenty-five dollars! Jo, I hope you haven't done anything rash?"

"No, it's mine honestly. I didn't beg, borrow, or steal it. I earned it, and I don't think you'll blame me, for I only sold what was my own."

As she spoke, Jo took off her bonnet, and a general outcry arose, for all her abundant hair was cut short.

"Your hair! Your beautiful hair!" "Oh, Jo, how could you? Your one beauty." "My dear girl, there was no need of this." "She doesn't look like my Jo any more, but I love her dearly for it!"

As everyone exclaimed, and Beth hugged the cropped head tenderly, Jo assumed an indifferent air, which did not deceive anyone a particle, and said, rumpling up the brown bush and trying to look as if she liked it, "It doesn't affect the fate of the nation, so don't wail, Beth. It will be good for my vanity, I was getting too proud of my wig. It will do my brains good to have that mop taken off. My head feels deliciously light and cool, and the barber said I could soon have a curly crop, which will be boyish, becoming, and easy to keep in order. I'm satisfied, so please take the money and let's have supper."

"Tell me all about it, Jo. I am not quite satisfied, but I can't blame you, for I know how willingly you sacrificed your vanity, as you call it, to your love. But, my dear, it was not necessary, and I'm afraid you will regret it one of these days," said Mrs. March.

"No, I won't!" returned Jo stoutly, feeling much relieved that her prank was not entirely condemned.

"What made you do it?" asked Amy, who would as soon have thought of cutting off her head as her pretty hair.

"Well, I was wild to do something for Father," replied Jo, as they gathered about the table, for healthy young people can eat even in the midst of trouble. "I hate to borrow as much as Mother does, and I knew Aunt March would croak, she always does, if you ask for a ninepence. Meg gave all her quarterly salary toward the rent, and I only got some clothes with mine, so I felt wicked, and was bound to have some money, if I sold the nose off my face to get it."

"You needn't feel wicked, my child! You had no winter things and got the simplest with your own hard earnings," said Mrs. March with a look that warmed Jo's heart.

"I hadn't the least idea of selling my hair at first, but as I went along I kept thinking what I could do, and feeling as if I'd like to dive into some of the rich stores and help myself. In a barber's window I saw tails of hair with the prices marked, and one black tail, not so thick as mine, was forty dollars. It came to me all of a sudden that I had one thing to make money out of, and without stopping to think, I walked in, asked if they bought hair, and what they would give for mine."

—From *Little Women*
by Louisa May Alcott

stop reading —■

You will now ask the student to summarize the passage in three sentences. To guide him towards a succinct summary, say, "Tell me what Jo did." His answer should resemble one of the following:

"Jo wanted to help her father, so she sold her hair to a barber. She gave the money to her mother. While the family had dinner, she told her mother and sisters about going to the barber shop."

"Jo had already spent her money on clothes, and she wanted to help her father. When she went past a barber shop, she saw hair for sale. So she went in and sold her hair, and gave the money to her mother."

"While Mrs. March was getting ready to go, Jo came in and brought twenty-five dollars. She had earned the money by selling her hair to a barber shop. She wanted to help her father, and she had already spent her money on clothes."

If the student has trouble choosing important details, ask these three questions:

What was the problem Jo faced?
How did she solve the problem?
What gave her the idea for this solution?

Write the narration down, but do not allow the student to watch. Then ask him whether he can repeat the first two sentences of the narration to himself. If not, read him the first two sentences. Tell him to listen carefully, since you will only read it once. Encourage him to repeat it to himself until he can remember it, and then to say it out loud to himself as he writes it down.

DAY TWO: Dictation

Tell the student that the following selection (from Chapter Sixteen of *Little Women*) is a single paragraph. A paragraph is a set of sentences organized around a single idea. Paragraphs are *indented*—the first line of the paragraph begins about five spaces from the margin.

Point out several paragraphs in the previous day's reading. Tell the student that the sentences in the dictation exercise all talk about one event—about Hannah, the housekeeper, making coffee for the girls to cheer them up after their mother leaves for Washington. Remind the student to indent the first line about five spaces.

Tell the student that you will read the selection three times. If necessary, you can prompt him a fourth time, but ask him to think hard first and try to "hear" the selection in his head. He can say the sentences out loud if he finds this helpful.

Be sure to pause at each comma, and to make a longer pause at the period.

> **Coffee was a treat, and Hannah showed great tact in making it that morning. No one could resist her persuasive nods, or the fragrant invitation issuing from the nose of the coffee pot.**

DAY THREE: Narration and Dictation

Allow the student to read the following story independently.

● — **begin reading** ————————————————————

THE SIEGE OF WASHINGTON, D.C.

This passage is from another book written about the Civil War, by a writer who lived at the same as Louisa May Alcott. His name was F. Colburn Adams. He was a soldier from Washington, D.C. Like the fictional Mr. March, he fought on the side of the North. He wrote The Siege of Washington, D.C. *so that children (including his own) could begin to understand the war. This book was written in 1867, only two years after the war had ended.*

You may find this passage difficult to read, because it was written a century and a half ago. Read it slowly. You may want to go back and read it a second time before you try to summarize it. You'll also be allowed to look back at the passage as you compose your summary.

The people of the South forgot all the great principles which govern humanity for humanity's good; they were betrayed into wrong doing by false friends, and made blind by their own prosperity. And they even forgot that God was their truest and best guardian, and to Him they must look for that care and protection which shall last forever.

But, my son, I would enjoin you to bear these people no ill will, and remember how much better it is in the sight of God to deal with the erring in the spirit of forgiveness. They were a brave and a gallant people, who fought in the belief that they were right, and with a heroism worthy of a good cause. It is only the meanest nature that has no respect for the courage and gallantry of an enemy, that cannot find in it something to admire. It was the selfishness, my son, which slavery begat in these people, that perverted their natures, and caused them to forget God.

Yes, my son, it was the curse of slavery that corrupted the hearts and turned the heads of these people. The Church might, and did, attempt to sanctify this greatest of crimes; but that did not change the character of the cruelty and injustice. It will, no doubt, seem strange to you that ministers of the Gospel should be found the defenders of crime. And yet slavery found its ablest defenders in the pulpit of the South.

I am afraid it always will be so, for even now we see ministers of the Gospel more ready to hang out false lights to lead their people into darkness, than to give them that truth and instruction they so much need. But you must not let the thought of this lessen your respect for the Church. Examine with great care until you have found out in what true Christianity consists; and when you have, practice accordingly to the extent of your ability.

But now I want to tell you, my son, how it was that the people of this great nation took to swords and cannon, to settle their differences of opinion.

The people of the great North, and the people of the great West, were educated to a very different way of thinking on the question of slavery, and differed with the people of the South. They were willing, for the sake of peace, to tolerate slavery, as a great evil it were dangerous to attempt to remove; but it was too much to ask them to accept it as a great national blessing. These people were energetic, thrifty, lovers of right and justice, and had grown rich and powerful by their own industry. They could not see why the whole people of so great a nation as ours should be required to bow down and worship what the rest of the civilized world had condemned as the greatest scourge of mankind.

Seeing the power this great wrong was obtaining over the nation, as well as the danger it was causing us by corrupting the minds of the people, they consulted together and elected a President after their own way of thinking. And this so offended the people of the South, who were a brave people, and quick to anger, that they gathered together from all parts of their country, gave up their peaceful pursuits, and went to war for what they called their independence. Yes, my son, these people scorned the example of the Christian world, went to war in defense of a great crime, and ceased only when they had destroyed themselves.

—Slightly condensed from *The Siege of Washington, D.C.*
by Captain F. Colburn Adams

stop reading →■

You will now ask the student to summarize the passage in three sentences. To guide him towards a succinct summary, say, "Why did fighting break out between North and South?" Allow him to look back at the passage while he writes.

His answer should resemble one of the following:

"The people of the South wanted to keep their slaves. The people of the North and West did not want to accept slavery. They elected a president who didn't want slavery, so the Southerners went to war."

"The people of the North and West tolerated slavery, but didn't approve of it. They elected a president who thought the same way they did. The people of the South went to war to defend slavery."

"The people of the South had slaves and didn't want to give them up. The people of the North and West elected a president who was against slavery. The people of the South were offended and went to war."

If the student has trouble choosing important details, ask these three questions:

What did the people of the South want?
What did the people of the North and West do that offended the South?
What was the South's response?

Write the narration down, but do not allow the student to watch. (Since the writer capitalizes the regional names North, South, and West, do the same as you write.) Then ask him whether he can repeat the first two sentences of the narration to himself. If not, read him the first two sentences. Tell him to listen carefully, since you will only read it once. Encourage him to repeat it to himself until he can remember it, and then to say it out loud to himself as he writes it down.

DAY FOUR: Dictation

Tell the student that the following selection is from Chapter IV of *The Siege of Washington, D.C.*, "The Battle of Bull-Run, and How it Ended." The chapter describes a famous battle, fought in Virginia near the beginning of the war. This selection is a paragraph about the condition of the Northern army. Remind the student to indent the first line of the paragraph.

Tell the student that you will read the selection three times. If necessary, you can prompt him a fourth time, but ask him to think hard first and try to "hear" the selection in his head. He can say the sentences out loud if he finds this helpful.

Be sure to pause at each comma, and to make a longer pause at the periods.

> **The morning was hot and sultry, and the air was misty with dust clouds. Our brave boys, who were not up to long marches, had a hard time of**

it. But they were full of patriotism, and bore up under it with great fortitude.

WEEKS 12–19

DAY ONE: Narration and Dictation

Choose reading passages of eight to ten paragraphs (roughly 40 to 45 lines) from the student's literature, science, or history texts. After the student reads the passage independently, ask him either to describe the scene, or to give you a brief narrative summary of the passage's events. Write the narration down, but do not allow the student to watch. Then ask him whether he can repeat the first two sentences of the narration to himself. If not, read him the first two sentences. Tell him to listen carefully, since you will only read the sentences once. Encourage him to repeat the sentences to himself until he can remember them, and then to say them out loud to himself as he writes.

DAY TWO: Dictation

Dictate selections of single short paragraphs (two or three sentences organized around a single idea; as you choose these, you can simply use the first two or three sentences of a longer paragraph). Remind the student that these are paragraphs, and that he should indent the first line.

Tell the student that you will read the selection three times. If necessary, you can prompt him a fourth time, but ask him to think hard first and try to "hear" the sentences in his head. He can say the sentences out loud if he finds this helpful.

Be sure to indicate any dialogue or unusual punctuation with your voice. If there are any unusual elements in the selection, tell the student to watch out for them.

Over these eight weeks, look for selections that include the following elements. Point them out to the student after he writes.

Possessives (e.g., whose, which, his) used both
as adjectives and pronouns .... Week 12
Adverbs .... Week 13
Helping verbs... Week 14

If you cannot find sentences that contain these elements, alternate choosing dictation sentences from the student's books and making up your own dictation sentences with these elements included; this will help the student to practice proper form.

DAY THREE: Narration and Dictation

Follow the narration and dictation guidelines above.

DAY FOUR: Dictation

Follow the dictation guidelines above.

Year Four, Weeks 20–27

Narration exercises will lengthen slightly to ten to twelve paragraphs. After reading the passage independently, the student will continue to answer a directed narration question with three or four sentences, and will write down the first two sentences of this narration for herself.

Dictation exercises will lengthen slightly to 25- 30-word paragraphs, repeated three times. You will also repeat the final sentence in these long dictations an additional time, if necessary.

The pattern of Week 20 will be followed in Weeks 21 through 27.

WEEK 20

DAY ONE: Narration and Dictation

Allow the student to read the following story independently.

●— begin reading ——————————————————————

"YOUNG BENJAMIN FRANKLIN"

Nathaniel Hawthorne was a nineteenth-century novelist who also wrote occasional stories for children.

When Benjamin Franklin was a boy he was very fond of fishing; and many of his leisure hours were spent on the margin of the mill pond catching flounders, perch, and eels that came up thither with the tide.

The place where Ben and his playmates did most of their fishing was a marshy spot on the outskirts of Boston. On the edge of the water there was a deep bed of clay, in which the boys were forced to stand while they caught their fish.

"This is very uncomfortable," said Ben Franklin one day to his comrades, while they were standing in the quagmire.

"So it is," said the other boys. "What a pity we have no better place to stand on!"

On the dry land, not far from the quagmire, there were at that time a great many large stones that had been brought there to be used in building the foundation of a new house. Ben mounted upon the highest of these stones.

"Boys," said he, "I have thought of a plan. You know what a plague it is to have to stand in the quagmire yonder. See, I am bedaubed to the knees, and you are all in the same plight.

"Now I propose that we build a wharf. You see these stones? The workmen mean to use them for building a house here. My plan is to take these same stones, carry them to the edge of the water, and build a wharf with them. What say you, lads? Shall we build the wharf?"

"Yes, yes," cried the boys; "let's set about it!"

It was agreed that they should all be on the spot that evening, and begin their grand public enterprise by moonlight.

Accordingly, at the appointed time, the boys met and eagerly began to remove the stones. They worked like a colony of ants, sometimes two or three of them taking hold of one stone; and at last they had carried them all away, and built their little wharf.

"Now, boys," cried Ben, when the job was done, "let's give three cheers, and go home to bed. To-morrow we may catch fish at our ease."

"Hurrah! hurrah! hurrah!" shouted his comrades, and all scampered off home and to bed, to dream of to-morrow's sport.

In the morning the masons came to begin their work. But what was their surprise to find the stones all gone! The master mason, looking carefully on the ground, saw the tracks of many little feet, some with shoes and some barefoot. Following these to the water side, he soon found what had become of the missing building stones.

"Ah! I see what the mischief is," said he; "those little rascals who were here yesterday have stolen the stones to build a wharf with. And I must say that they understand their business well."

He was so angry that he at once went to make a complaint before the magistrate; and his Honor wrote an order to "take the bodies of Benjamin Franklin, and other evil-disposed persons," who had stolen a heap of stones.

If the owner of the stolen property had not been more merciful than the master mason, it might have gone hard with our friend Benjamin and his comrades. But, luckily for them, the gentleman had a respect for Ben's father, and, moreover, was pleased with the spirit of the whole affair. He therefore let the culprits off easily.

But the poor boys had to go through another trial, and receive sentence, and suffer punishment, too, from their own fathers. Many a rod was worn to the stump on that unlucky night. As for Ben, he was less afraid of a whipping than of his father's reproof. And, indeed, his father was very much disturbed.

"Benjamin, come hither," began Mr. Franklin in his usual stern and weighty tone. The boy approached and stood before his father's chair. "Benjamin," said his father, "what could induce you to take property which did not belong to you?"

"Why, father," replied Ben, hanging his head at first, but then lifting his eyes to Mr. Franklin's face, "if it had been merely for my own benefit, I never should have dreamed of it. But I knew that the wharf would be a public convenience. If the owner of the stones should build a house with them, nobody would enjoy any advantage but himself. Now, I made use of them in a way that was for the advantage of many persons."

"My son," said Mr. Franklin solemnly, "so far as it was in your power, you have done a greater harm to the public than to the owner of the stones. I do verily believe, Benjamin, that almost all the public and private misery of mankind arises from a neglect of this great truth— that evil can produce only evil, that good ends must be wrought out by good means."

To the end of his life, Ben Franklin never forgot this conversation with his father; and we have reason to suppose, that, in most of his public and private career, he sought to act upon the principles which that good and wise man then taught him.

—From *The Fourth McGuffey Reader*
ed. by William H McGuffey

———————————————— **stop reading** →■

You will now ask the student to summarize the passage in three or four sentences. To guide her towards a succinct summary, say, "Tell me about Benjamin Franklin's attempt to build a wharf." Her answer should resemble one of the following:

> "Benjamin Franklin and his friends wanted to build a wharf. They used a nearby pile of stones that belonged to someone else. When their parents found out they had stolen the stones, they all got into trouble. Franklin said that stealing the stones was all right, because the wharf could be used by everyone, but his father told him that it was still wrong."

> "Benjamin Franklin and his friends were tired of standing in the mud to fish. They used a nearby pile of stones to build a wharf. But the owner of the stones complained to their parents, and they were all punished. Franklin learned that stealing was evil, even if it was done for the advantage of others."

> "Benjamin Franklin and his friends used someone else's stones to build a wharf. They almost got arrested, and their parents punished them. Benjamin Franklin said that it was all right to take the stones, because the wharf could be used by everyone, and the owner of the stones was going to use them only for himself. But his father told him that he should never do evil in order to bring about something good."

If the student has trouble choosing important details, ask these three questions:

What did Franklin and his friends do?
Why did this get them into trouble?
What was Franklin's excuse and his father's response?

Write the narration down, but do not allow the student to watch. Then ask her whether she can repeat the first two sentences of the narration to herself. If not, read her the first two sentences. Tell her to listen carefully, since you will only read it once. Encourage her to repeat it to herself until she can remember it, and then to say it out loud to herself as she writes it down.

DAY TWO: Dictation

Tell the student that Hawthorne's story is based on a single paragraph in Benjamin Franklin's autobiography, which he wrote himself and finished in 1771. Read this entire paragraph as the student listens. You will probably want to tell the student that "emmet" is an old word for "ant":

> There was a salt-marsh that bounded part of the mill-pond, on the edge of which, at high water, we used to stand to fish for minnows. By much trampling, we had made it a mere quagmire. My proposal was to build a wharf there fit for us to stand upon, and I showed my comrades a large heap of stones, which were intended for a new house near the marsh, and which would very well suit our purpose. Accordingly, in the evening, when the workmen were gone, I assembled a number of my play-fellows, and working with them diligently like so many emmets, sometimes two or three to a stone, we brought

them all away and built our little wharf. The next morning
the workmen were surprised at missing the stones, which were
found in our wharf. Inquiry was made after the removers; we
were discovered and complained of; several of us were corrected
by our fathers; and though I pleaded the usefulness of the
work, mine convinced me that nothing was useful which was
not honest.

—From *The Autobiography of Benjamin Franklin*
by Benjamin Franklin

You may want to discuss with the student how much of Hawthorne's version was simply made up out of his own head so that it would be more interesting!

When you are finished, tell the student that you will be challenging her with a longer dictation than usual. Remind her that this is a paragraph (all of the sentences center around the topic of the wharf in the marsh) and that the first line should be indented.

Tell the student that you will read the selection three times. You will then ask her to write as much of it as she can remember. If she gets stuck, you will read the passage again from the point where her memory failed—but you'll only do this once!

Before you read, tell the student to write the following words on another piece of paper. Each word is hyphenated: *salt-marsh*, *mill-pond*.

Be sure to pause at each comma, and to make a longer pause at the periods.

There was a salt-marsh that bounded part of the mill-pond, on the edge of which, at high water, we used to stand to fish for minnows. By much trampling, we had made it a mere quagmire. My proposal was to build a wharf there fit for us to stand upon, and I showed my comrades a large heap of stones, which were intended for a new house near the marsh, and which would very well suit our purpose.

DAY THREE: Narration and Dictation

Allow the student to read the following story independently.

● — **begin reading** ———————————————————

"THE WHISTLE"

James Baldwin was a teacher who lived 1841–1925. He wrote many books for his young students. This tale is from one of those books. It is an interesting story—but Baldwin probably invented it, since it isn't in Benjamin Franklin's autobiography at all!

Two hundred years ago there lived in Boston a little boy whose name was Benjamin Franklin.

On the day that he was seven years old, his mother gave him a few pennies. He looked at the bright, yellow pieces and said, "What shall I do with these coppers, mother?" It was the first money that he had ever had.

"You may buy something, if you wish," said his mother.

"And then will you give me more?" he asked.

His mother shook her head and said: "No, Benjamin. I cannot give you any more. So you must be careful not to spend these foolishly."

The little fellow ran into the street. He heard the pennies jingle in his pocket. How rich he was!

Boston is now a great city, but at that time it was only a little town. There were not many stores.

As Benjamin ran down the street, he wondered what he should buy. Should he buy candy? He hardly knew how it tasted. Should he buy a pretty toy? If he had been the only child in the family, things might have been different. But there were fourteen boys and girls older than he, and two little sisters who were younger.

What a big family it was! And the father was a poor man. No wonder the lad had never owned a toy.

He had not gone far when he met a larger boy, who was blowing a whistle.

"I wish I had that whistle," he said.

The big boy looked at him and blew it again. Oh, what a pretty sound it made!

"I have some pennies," said Benjamin. He held them in his hand, and showed them to the boy. "You may have them, if you will give me the whistle."

"All of them?"

"Yes, all of them."

"Well, it's a bargain," said the boy; and he gave the whistle to Benjamin, and took the pennies.

Little Benjamin Franklin was very happy; for he was only seven years old. He ran home as fast as he could, blowing the whistle as he ran.

"See, mother," he said, "I have bought a whistle."

"How much did you pay for it?"

"All the pennies you gave me."

"Oh, Benjamin!"

One of his brothers asked to see the whistle.

"Well, well!" he said. "You've paid a dear price for this thing. It's only a penny whistle, and a poor one at that."

"You might have bought half a dozen such whistles with the money I gave you," said his mother.

The little boy saw what a mistake he had made. The whistle did not please him any more. He threw it upon the floor and began to cry.

"Never mind, my child," said his mother, very kindly. "You are only a very little boy, and you will learn a great deal as you grow bigger. The lesson you have learned to-day is never to pay too dear for a whistle."

Benjamin Franklin lived to be a very old man, but he never forgot that lesson.

Every boy and girl should remember the name of Benjamin Franklin. He was a great thinker and a great doer, and with Washington he helped to make our country free. His life was such that no man could ever say, "Ben Franklin has wronged me."

"The Whistle" From *Fifty Famous People,*
by James Baldwin

stop reading ▸

You will now ask the student, "Can you tell me about Benjamin Franklin and the penny whistle in three sentences?" The student's narration should resemble one of the following (and there should be no reason for the student to need a fourth sentence):

> "When Benjamin Franklin was little, his mother gave him some pennies. He met a boy with a whistle, and gave the boy all of his pennies for it. When he went home, he discovered that the whistle was only worth one penny."

> "Benjamin Franklin's mother gave him a handful of pennies. He set off to buy a toy. When he saw a boy playing a whistle, he bought it with all of his money—even though it was only worth one penny."

> "When he was seven years old, Benjamin Franklin got a few pennies from his mother. He knew that he could buy something exciting with it—like candy or a toy. But then he saw a boy playing a penny whistle, and he wanted it so much that he spent all of his money for it."

If the student has trouble choosing important details, ask these three questions:

What did Franklin get from his mother?
What did he buy?
Why was this a problem?

Write the narration down, but do not allow the student to watch. Then ask her whether she can repeat the first two sentences of the narration to herself. If not, read her the first two sentences. Tell her to listen carefully, since you will only read it once. Encourage her to repeat it to herself until she can remember it, and then to say it out loud to herself as she writes it down.

DAY FOUR: Dictation

Tell the student that the following passage from Franklin's autobiography is the only information *he* gives us about his childhood spending habits. Before you give the student her dictation assignment, read this entire selection aloud. You may wish to tell the student that a book of "polemic divinity" is a book that argues for a particular theological belief.

> From a child I was fond of reading, and all the little money that came into my hands was ever laid out in books. Pleased with the *Pilgrim's Progress*, my first collection was of John Bunyan's works in separate little volumes. I afterward sold them to enable me to buy R. Burton's Historical Collections; they were small chapmen's books, and cheap, 40 or 50 in all. My father's little library consisted chiefly of books in polemic divinity, most of which I read....Plutarch's Lives there was in which I read abundantly, and I still think that time spent to great advantage. There was also a book of [Daniel] Defoe's, called an *Essay on Projects*, and another of Dr. Mather's, called *Essays to do Good*, which perhaps gave me a turn of thinking that had an influence on some of the principal future events of my life. This bookish inclination at length determined my father to make me a printer....
>
> —From *The Autobiography of Benjamin Franklin*
> by Benjamin Franklin

Now prepare the student to take the following sentences from dictation. Remind her that this is a paragraph and that the first line should be indented.

Tell the student that you will read the selection three times, but you won't read it a fourth time—it's shorter than the last dictation exercise.

Before you dictate, remind the student that *Pilgrim's Progress* is the title of a book, and so should be underlined.

Be sure to pause at each comma, and to make a longer pause at the periods.

> From a child I was fond of reading, and all
> the little money that came into my hands was
> ever laid out in books. Pleased with the <u>Pilgrim's
> Progress</u>, my first collection was of John Bunyan's
> works in separate little volumes.

WEEKS 21–27

DAY ONE: Narration and Dictation

Choose reading passages of ten to twelve paragraphs (roughly 55 to 75 lines) from the student's literature, science, or history texts. After the student reads the passage independently, ask her either to describe the scene, or to give you a brief narrative summary of the passage's events in three or four sentences.

Write the narration down, but do not allow the student to watch. Then ask her whether she can repeat the first two sentences of the narration to herself. If not, read her the first two sentences. Tell her to listen carefully, since you will only read the sentences once. Encourage her to repeat the sentences to herself until she can remember them, and then to say them out loud to herself as she writes.

DAY TWO: Dictation

Dictate selections of single paragraphs, 25 to 30 words in length. Remind the student that these are paragraphs, and that she should indent the first line.

Tell the student that you will read the selection three times. If necessary, you can prompt her a fourth time, but ask her to think hard first and try to "hear" the sentences in her head. She can say the sentences out loud if she finds this helpful.

Be sure to indicate any dialogue or unusual punctuation with your voice. If there are any unusual elements in the selection, tell the student to watch out for them.

Over these seven weeks, look for selections that include the following elements. Point them out to the student after she writes.

Commands .... Week 21

Questions .... Week 22

Prepositions, prepositional phrases, objects of the preposition .... Weeks 23–24

Abbreviations (titles of respect, measurements, streets, initials) .... Week 25

Commas in a series...................................... Week 26

Commas after yes, no, or terms of direct address .... Week 27

If you cannot find sentences that contain these elements, alternate choosing dictation sentences from the student's books and making up your own dictation sentences with these elements included; this will help the student to practice proper form.

DAY THREE: Narration and Dictation
Follow the narration and dictation guidelines above.

DAY FOUR: Dictation
Follow the dictation guidelines above.

Year Four, Weeks 28–35

Narration exercises will remain at ten to twelve paragraphs, but after reading the passage independently, the student will answer the more general question "What is this passage about?" with a three- or four-sentence narration. During this final step, the student will move away from the need for directed narration, and will begin to learn to identify for himself what type of narration is necessary. After composing his narration exercise orally, the student will write it down himself.

Dictation exercises will remain 25- to 30-word paragraphs, repeated three times. The pattern of Week 28 will be followed in Weeks 29 through 35.

WEEK 28

DAY ONE: Narration and Dictation

Allow the student to read the following passage independently.

●— **begin reading** ─────────────────────────────

Daniel Defoe, the writer that Benjamin Franklin mentions in his autobiography, lived from around 1661 to 1731. His most famous book, Robinson Crusoe, *tells the story of a man who is cast away all alone on a desert island. In this passage, Robinson Crusoe and his shipmates have escaped from their sinking ship and are in the lifeboat, trying to get to shore.*

You may find this passage challenging to read—but take your time and read it more than once if necessary. You will be allowed to look back at it while you write your summary!

And now our case was very dismal indeed; for we all saw plainly, that the sea went so high, that the boat could not live, and that we should be inevitably drowned. As to making sail, we had none, nor, if we had, could we have done any thing with it; so we worked at the oar towards the land, though with heavy hearts, like men going to execution; for we all knew, that when the boat came nearer the shore, she would be dashed into a thousand pieces by the breach of the sea. However, we committed our souls to God in the most earnest manner; and the wind driving us towards the shore, we hastened our destruction with our own hands, pulling as well as we could towards land.

What the shore was, whether rock or sand, whether steep or shoal, we knew not; the only hope that could rationally give us the least shadow of expectation, was, if we might happen into some bay or gulf, or the mouth of some river, where, by great chance, we might have run our boat in, or got under the lee of the land, and perhaps made smooth water. But there was nothing of this appeared; but as we made nearer and nearer the shore, the land looked more frightful than the sea.

After we had rowed, or rather driven about a league and a half, as we reckoned it, a raging wave, mountain-like, came rolling astern of us, and plainly had us expect the coup-de-grace. In a word, it took us with such a fury, that it overset the boat at once; and separating us as well from the boat, as from one another, gave us not time hardly to say O God! for we were all swallowed up in a moment.

Nothing can describe the confusion of thought which I felt when I sunk into the water; for though I swam very well, yet I could not deliver myself from the waves so as to draw breath, till that wave having driven me, or rather carried me a vast way on towards the shore, and having spent itself, went back, and left me upon the land almost dry, but half dead with the water I took in. I had so much presence of mind as well as breath left, that, seeing myself nearer the main land than I expected, I got upon my feet, and endeavoured to make on towards the land as fast as I could, before another wave should return, and take me up again.

But I soon found it was impossible to avoid it; for I saw the sea come after me as high as a great hill, and as furious as an enemy which I had no means or strength to contend with; my business was to hold my breath, and raise myself upon the water, if I could; and so by swimming to preserve my breathing, and pilot myself towards the shore, if possible; my greatest concern now being, that the sea, as it would carry me a great way towards the shore when it came on, might not carry me back again with it when it gave back towards the sea.

The wave that came upon me again, buried me at once twenty or thirty foot deep in its own body; and I could feel myself carried with a mighty force and swiftness towards the shore a very great way; but I held my breath, and assisted myself to swim still forward with all my might. I was ready to burst with holding my breath, when, as I felt myself rising up, so, to my immediate relief, I found my head and hands shoot out above the surface of the water; and though it was not two seconds of time that I could keep myself so, yet it relieved me greatly, gave me breath and new courage. I was covered again with water a good while, but not so long but I held it out; and finding the water had spent itself, and began to return, I struck forward against the return of the waves, and felt ground again with my feet.

I stood still a few moments to recover breath, and till the water went from me, and then took to my heels, and ran with what strength I had farther towards the shore. But neither would this deliver me from the fury of the sea, which came pouring in after me again; and twice more I was lifted up by the waves and carried forwards as before, the shore being very flat.

The last time of these two had well near been fatal to me; for the sea having hurried me along as before, landed me, or rather dashed me against a piece of a rock, and that with such force, as it left me senseless, and indeed helpless, as to my own deliverance; for the blow taking my side and breast, beat the breath as it were quite out of my body; and had it returned again immediately, I must have been strangled in the water; but I recovered a little before the return of the waves, and seeing I should be covered again with the water, I resolved to hold fast by a piece of the rock, and so to hold my breath, if possible, till the wave went back.

Now as the waves were not so high as at first, being near land, I held my hold till the wave abated, and then fetched another run, which brought me so near the shore, that the next wave, though it went over me, yet did not so swallow me up as to carry me away; and the next run I took I got to the main land, where, to my great comfort, I clambered up the cliffs of the shore, and sat me down upon the grass, free from danger, and quite out of the reach of the water.

—From *The Life and Adventures of Robinson Crusoe*
by Daniel Defoe

stop reading ⟶◾

You will now ask the student to summarize the passage in three or four sentences, and then to repeat that narration to himself and write it down. Prepare him for this by giving him a choice: you can write the narration down for reference, and then help him repeat it to himself as he writes; or he can tell his narration to a tape recorder and then play the tape recorder back as he writes. (He may not need either of these aids; if he simply wants to write, allow him to do so.)

Rather than directing his narration, simply say, "What is this passage about?" His answer should resemble one of the following:

> "Robinson Crusoe and the other sailors tried to row the boat towards shore. A huge wave turned the boat over, and Crusoe was thrown up onto the land. But another wave tried to pull him back into the sea. He was almost smashed against a rock, but managed to hold on to it and climb up to dry land."

> "Robinson Crusoe was thrown into the ocean by a huge wave. He was carried up onto the shore, but then another enormous wave buried him. He was afraid that he would be drowned or dashed to death against the rocks, but finally he managed to pull himself out of the reach of the water."

> "Robinson Crusoe was shipwrecked with his companions, but a wave overturned their lifeboat. Crusoe tried to get to land, but waves kept pulling him back into the sea. Finally he managed to hold onto a rock long enough to get free of the water. Then he ran for dry land."

Give the student a chance to come up with his own narration. However, if the student has difficulty with the narration, you can assist him by saying, "How did Robinson Crusoe get to dry land?"

Day Two: Dictation

Tell the student that this following paragraph comes from later in the book, after Robinson Crusoe has been shipwrecked for nearly a year.

Remind him to indent the first sentence. Repeat the selection three times. Only prompt the student a fourth time if he becomes completely stalled.

Be sure to pause at each comma, and to make a longer pause at the period.

> I had been now in this unhappy island above ten months. All possibility of deliverance from this condition seemed to be entirely taken from me, and I firmly believed that no human person had ever set foot upon that place.

DAY THREE: Narration Writing

Allow the student to read the following passage independently.

●── **begin reading** ──────────────────────────────

"THE STORY OF A GREAT STORY"

Like the story of Benjamin Franklin, this story was written for young students by the teacher James Baldwin. However, this particular story is based in fact.

You will notice how much simpler the language is in this story. Daniel Defore wrote his story for everyone; Baldwin is writing for children. Which kind of writing do you like better?

Two hundred years ago there lived in Scotland a young man whose name was Alexander Selkirk. He was quarrelsome and unruly. He was often making trouble among his neighbors. For this reason many people were glad when he ran away from home and went to sea. "We hope that he will get what he deserves," they said.

He was big and strong and soon became a fine sailor. But he was still headstrong and ill-tempered; and he was often in trouble with the other sailors.

Once his ship was sailing in the great Pacific Ocean. It was four hundred miles from the coast of South America. Then something happened which Selkirk did not like. He became very disagreeable. He quarreled with the other sailors, and even with the captain.

"I would rather live alone on a desert island than be a sailor on this ship," he said.

"Very well," answered the captain. "We shall put you ashore on the first island that we see."

"Do so," said Selkirk. "You cannot please me better."

The very next day they came in sight of a little green island. There were groves of trees near the shore, and high hills beyond them.

"What is the name of this island?" asked Selkirk.

"Juan Fernandez," said the captain.

"Set me on shore and leave me there. Give me a few common tools and some food, and I will do well enough," said the sailor.

"It shall be done," answered the captain.

So they filled a small boat with the things that he would need the most—an ax, a hoe, a kettle, and some other things. They also put in some bread and meat and other food, enough for several weeks. Then four of the sailors rowed him to the shore and left him there.

Alexander Selkirk was all alone on the island. He began to see how foolish he had been; he thought how terrible it would be to live there without one friend, without one person to whom he could speak.

He called loudly to the sailors and to the captain.

"Oh, do not leave me here. Take me back, and I will give

you no more trouble." But they would not listen to him. The ship sailed away and was soon lost to sight.

Then Selkirk set to work to make the best of things. He built him a little hut for shelter at night and in stormy weather. He planted a small garden. There were pigs and goats on the island, and plenty of fish could be caught from the shore. So there was always plenty of food. Sometimes Selkirk saw ships sailing in the distance. He tried to make signals to them; he called as loudly as he could; but he was neither seen nor heard, and the ships came no nearer.

"If I ever have the good fortune to escape from this island," he said, "I will be kind and obliging to every one. I will try to make friends instead of enemies."

For four years and four months he lived alone on the island. Then, to his great joy, a ship came near and anchored in the little harbor. He made himself known, and the captain willingly agreed to carry him back to his own country. When he reached Scotland everybody was eager to hear him tell of his adventures, and he soon found himself famous.

In England there was then living a man whose name was Daniel Defoe. He was a writer of books. He had written many stories which people at that time liked to read. When Daniel Defoe heard how Selkirk had lived alone on the island of Juan Fernandez, he said to himself: "Here is something worth telling about. The story of Alexander Selkirk is very pleasing."

So he sat down and wrote a wonderful story, which he called "The Adventures of Robinson Crusoe." Every boy has heard of Robinson Crusoe. Many boys and indeed many girls have read his story.

Here is the story: When only a child, Robinson Crusoe liked to stand by the river and see the ships sailing past. He wondered where they had come from and where they were going. He talked with some of the sailors. They told him about the strange lands they had visited far over the sea. They told him about the wonderful things they had seen there. He was delighted.

"Oh, I wish I could be a sailor!" he said.

He could not think of anything else. He thought how grand it would be to sail and sail on the wide blue sea. He thought how pleasant it would be to visit strange countries and see strange peoples.

As he grew up, his father wished him to learn a trade. "No, no, I am going to be a sailor; I am going to see the world," he said.

His mother said to him: "A sailor's life is a hard life. There are great storms on the sea. Many ships are wrecked and the sailors are drowned."

"I am not afraid," said Robinson Crusoe. "I am going to be a sailor and nothing else." So, when he was eighteen years old, he ran away from his pleasant home and went to sea.

He soon found that his mother's words were true. A sailor's life is indeed a hard life. There is no time to play. Every day there is much work to be done. Sometimes there is great danger.

Robinson Crusoe sailed first on one ship and then on another. He visited many lands and saw many wonderful things.

One day there was a great storm. The ship was driven about by the winds; it was wrecked. All the sailors were drowned but Robinson Crusoe.

He swam to an island that was not far away. It was a small island, and there was no one living on it. But there were birds in the woods and some wild goats on the hills.

For a long time Robinson Crusoe was all alone. He had only a dog and some cats to keep him company. Then he tamed a parrot and some goats. He built a house of some sticks and vines. He sowed grain and baked bread. He made a boat for himself. He did a great many things. He was busy every day. At last a ship happened to pass that way and Robinson was taken on board. He was glad to go back to England to see his home and his friends once more.

This is the story which Mr. Defoe wrote. Perhaps he would not have thought of it, had he not first heard the true story of Alexander Selkirk.

— From *Fifty Famous People*
by James Baldwin

stop reading ➞■

You will now ask the student to summarize the passage in three or four sentences, and then to repeat that narration to himself and write it down. Use the same techniques suggested above.

Rather than directing his narration, simply say, "What is this passage about? Remember that you only need to tell me about Alexander Selkirk— you don't need to tell me the plot of Robinson Crusoe." His answer should resemble one of the following:

> "The story of Robinson Crusoe was based on the life of Alexander Selkirk. He was a troublemaker who ran away to sea. When he had an argument with his captain, he asked to be put on a desert island. He stayed on the island four years and four months."

> "Alexander Selkirk lived in Scotland two hundred years ago. He became a sailor, but he didn't get along with his captain. He was put on a desert island with food and a few tools and left there alone. He built a hut, planted a garden, and lived there for four and a half years."

> "Alexander Selkirk was a sailor whose captain put him ashore on a desert island. Selkirk tried to make signals to passing ships, but he remained alone on the island for four years and four months. Daniel Defore used his story to write *Robinson Crusoe.*"

Give the student a chance to come up with his own narration. However, if the student has difficulty with the narration, you can assist him by saying,

"How did Alexander Selkirk get on and off the desert island?"

If the student uses the title of the book *Robinson Crusoe*, remind him to underline it.

DAY FOUR: Dictation

Tell the student that Alexander Selkirk remained on his island, all alone, for four years. After he was rescued and returned to England, a newspaper reporter named Richard Steele interviewed him and published an article about him. The dictation sentences for today come from the article, which first ran on December 1, 1713. Selkirk was put ashore with only enough food for two meals, and found that the island was mostly populated with goats, wild cats, and rats, none of which he wanted to eat.

Here is the dictation exercise. (Spelling and capitalization has been regularized for the purposes of dictation) Read it three times and ask the student to write as much as he can from memory. When he gets stuck, you can repeat the selection. This is a difficult assignment, so give the student any help needed.

> He judged it most probable that he should find more immediate and easy relief, by finding shellfish on the shore, than seeking game with his gun. He accordingly found great quantities of turtles, whose flesh is extremely delicious, and of which he frequently ate very plentifully on his first arrival, till it grew disagreeable to his stomach, except in jellies.

WEEKS 29–35

DAY ONE: Narration and Dictation

Choose reading passages of ten to twelve paragraphs (roughly 55 to 75 lines) from the student's literature, science, or history texts. After the student reads the passage independently, ask him either to describe the scene, or to give you a brief narrative summary of the passage's events in three or four sentences. He should write this narration down himself; give him any necessary help in spelling and punctuation.

Day Two: Dictation

Dictate selections of single paragraphs, 25 to 30 words in length. Remind the student that these are paragraphs, and that he should indent the first line. Tell the student that you will read the selection three times. If necessary, you can prompt him a fourth time, but ask him to think hard first and try to "hear" the sentences in his head. He can say the sentences out loud if he finds this helpful.

Be sure to indicate any dialogue or unusual punctuation with your voice. If there are any unusual elements in the selection, tell the student to watch out for them.

Over these seven weeks, look for selections that include the following elements. Point them out to the student after he writes.

Contractions .... Week 29
Direct quotations .... Weeks 30–31
Interjections .... Week 32
Compound subjects and verbs .... Week 33
Compound sentences with semicolons .... Week 34
Comparative and superlative adjectives .... Week 35

If you cannot find sentences that contain these elements, alternate choosing dictation sentences from the student's books and making up your own dictation sentences with these elements included; this will help the student to practice proper form.

Day Three: Narration Writing
Follow the narration and dictation guidelines above.

Day Four: Dictation
Follow the dictation guidelines above.

Year Four Mastery Evaluation, Week 36

By this point, the student should be able to read a passage independently, sum it up in three or four sentences, write those sentences down (with some assistance if necessary), and take dictation exercises of around 25 to 30 words after three to four repetitions.

If the student struggles with any of these skills in the evaluation that follows, plan on spending a few more weeks on either dictation or narration in order to provide extra practice.

NARRATION EVALUATION

Give the following passage to the student to read independently.

●— **begin reading** ——————————————————————

This book, which was first published in 1877, tells the story of a beautiful horse who begins life as a carefree colt. Later, Black Beauty is sold and goes through many adventures and difficulties.

These are the first two chapters of Black Beauty. *After you read each chapter, summarize it in two to three sentences, and write those sentences down. Be sure to indent the first line of each summary.*

You may look back at the story while you are working on your summary.

CHAPTER ONE: MY EARLY HOME

The first place that I can well remember was a large pleasant meadow with a pond of clear water in it. Some shady trees leaned over it, and rushes and water-lilies grew at the deep end. Over the hedge on one side we looked into a plowed field, and on the other we looked over a gate at our master's house, which stood by the roadside; at the top of the meadow was a grove of fir trees, and at the bottom a running brook overhung by a steep bank.

While I was young I lived upon my mother's milk, as I could not eat grass. In the daytime I ran by her side, and at night I lay down close by her. When it was hot we used to stand by the pond in the shade of the trees, and when it was cold we had a nice warm shed near the grove.

As soon as I was old enough to eat grass my mother used to go out to work in the daytime, and come back in the evening.

There were six young colts in the meadow besides me; they were older than I was; some were nearly as large as grown-up horses. I used to run with them, and had great fun; we used to gallop all together round and round the field as hard as we could go. Sometimes we had rather rough play, for they would frequently bite and kick as well as gallop.

One day, when there was a good deal of kicking, my mother whinnied to me to come to her, and then she said:

"I wish you to pay attention to what I am going to say to you. The colts who live here are very good colts, but they are cart-horse colts, and of course they have not learned manners. You have been well-bred and well-born; your father has a great name in these parts, and your grandfather won the cup two years at the Newmarket races; your grandmother had the sweetest temper of any horse I ever knew, and I think you have never seen me kick or bite. I hope you will grow up gentle and good, and never learn bad ways; do your work with a good will, lift your feet up well when you trot, and never bite or kick even in play."

I have never forgotten my mother's advice; I knew she was a wise old horse, and our master thought a great deal of her. Her name was Duchess, but he often called her Pet.

Our master was a good, kind man. He gave us good food, good lodging, and kind words; he spoke as kindly to us as he did to his little children. We were all fond of him, and my mother loved him very much. When she saw him at the gate she would neigh with joy, and trot up to him. He would pat and stroke her and say, "Well, old Pet, and how is your little Beauty?" Then he would give me a piece of bread, which was very good, and sometimes he brought a carrot for my mother. All the horses would come to him, but I think we were his favorites. My mother always took him to the town on a market day in a light gig.

There was a plowboy, Dick, who sometimes came into our field to pluck blackberries from the hedge. When he had eaten all he wanted he would have what he called fun with the colts, throwing stones and sticks at them to make them gallop. We did not much mind him, for we could gallop off; but sometimes a stone would hit and hurt us.

One day he was at this game, and did not know that the master was in the next field; but he was there, watching what was going on; over the hedge he jumped in a snap, and catching Dick by the arm, he gave him such a box on the ear as made him roar with the pain and surprise. As soon as we saw the master we trotted up nearer to see what went on.

"Bad boy!" he said, "bad boy! to chase the colts. This is not the first time, nor the second, but it shall be the last. There—take your money and go home; I shall not want you on my farm again." So we never saw Dick any more. Old Daniel, the man who looked after the horses, was just as gentle as our master, so we were well off.

Chapter Two: The Hunt

Before I was two years old a circumstance happened which I have never forgotten. It was early in the spring; there had been a little frost in the night, and a light mist still hung over the woods and meadows. I and the other colts were feeding at the lower part of the field when we heard, quite in the distance, what sounded like the cry of dogs. The oldest of the colts raised his head, pricked his ears, and said, "There are the hounds!" and immediately cantered off, followed by the rest of us to the upper part of the field, where we could look over the hedge and see several fields beyond. My mother and an old riding horse of our master's were also standing near, and seemed to know all about it.

"They have found a hare," said my mother, "and if they come this way we shall see the hunt."

And soon the dogs were all tearing down the field of young wheat next to ours. I never heard such a noise as they made. They did not bark, nor howl, nor whine, but kept on a "yo! yo, o, o! yo! yo, o, o!" at the top of their voices. After them came a number of men on horseback, some of them in green coats, all galloping as fast as they could. The old horse snorted and looked eagerly after them, and we young colts wanted to be galloping with them, but they were soon away into the fields lower down; here it seemed as if they had come to a stand; the dogs left off barking, and ran about every way with their noses to the ground.

"They have lost the scent," said the old horse; "perhaps the hare will get off."

"What hare?" I said.

"Oh! I don't know what hare; likely enough it may be one of our own hares out of the woods; any hare they can find will do for the dogs and men to run after;" and before long the dogs began their "yo! yo, o, o!" again, and back they came altogether at full speed, making straight for our meadow at the part where the high bank and hedge overhang the brook.

"Now we shall see the hare," said my mother; and just then a hare wild with fright rushed by and made for the woods. On came the dogs; they burst over the bank, leaped the stream, and came dashing across the field followed by the huntsmen. Six or eight men leaped their horses clean over, close upon the dogs. The hare tried to get through the fence; it was too thick, and she turned sharp round to make for the road, but it was too late; the dogs were upon her with their wild cries; we heard one shriek, and that was the end of her. One of the huntsmen rode up and whipped off the dogs, who would soon have torn her to pieces. He held her up by the leg torn and bleeding, and all the gentlemen seemed well pleased.

As for me, I was so astonished that I did not at first see what was going on by the brook; but when I did look there was a sad sight; two fine horses were down, one was struggling in the stream, and the other was groaning on the grass. One of the riders was getting out of the water covered with mud, the other lay quite still.

"His neck is broke," said my mother.

"And serve him right, too," said one of the colts.

I thought the same, but my mother did not join with us.

"Well, no," she said, "you must not say that; but though I am an old horse, and have seen and heard a great deal, I never yet could make out why men are so fond of this sport; they often hurt themselves, often spoil good horses, and tear up the fields, and all for a hare or a fox, or a stag, that they could get more easily some other way; but we are only horses, and don't know."

While my mother was saying this we stood and looked on. Many of the riders had gone to the young man; but my master, who had been watching what was going on, was the first to raise him. His head fell back and his arms hung down, and every one looked very serious. There was no noise now; even the dogs were quiet, and seemed to know that something was wrong. They carried him to our master's house. I heard afterward that it was young George Gordon, the squire's only son, a fine, tall young man, and the pride of his family.

There was now riding off in all directions to the doctor's, to the farrier's, and no doubt to Squire Gordon's, to let him know about his son. When Mr. Bond, the farrier, came to look at the black horse that lay groaning on the grass, he felt him all over, and shook his head; one of his legs was broken. Then some one ran to our master's house and came back with a gun; presently there was a loud bang and a dreadful shriek, and then all was still; the black horse moved no more.

My mother seemed much troubled; she said she had known that horse for years, and that his name was "Rob Roy"; he was a good horse, and there was no vice in him. She never would go to that part of the field afterward.

Not many days after we heard the church-bell tolling for a long time, and looking over the gate we saw a long, strange black coach that was covered with black cloth and was drawn by black horses; after that came another and another and another, and all were black, while the bell kept tolling, tolling. They were carrying young Gordon to the churchyard to bury him. He would never ride again. What they did with Rob Roy I never knew; but 'twas all for one little hare.

—From *Black Beauty: The Autobiography of a Horse*
by Anna Sewell

stop reading →■

The student's final set of summaries should resemble one of the following. Remember, it is perfectly fine for you to help with spelling and punctuation.

"Black Beauty first lived in a large meadow with his mother and six other colts. His master was a kind, good man who protected his horses from being chased or frightened."

"When he was young, he saw men on horseback, going out hunting. They were chasing a hare, when two of the horses fell. One of the riders was killed."

"When Black Beauty was little, he lived with his mother, who taught him not to kick and bite. He had plenty of playmates, and his master was kind to him."

"One day, he saw dogs and hunters out chasing a hare. The hare was killed, but during the hunt, one of the hunters was also killed. He was buried in a churchyard near the field."

DICTATION EVALUATION

Tell the student that the following paragraph comes from Chapter Four, "Birtwick Park," in which Black Beauty goes to his new home. You will read the selection three times, and you will prompt the student one more time if necessary.

Remind the student that quotation marks go around dialogue, and that the ending punctuation marks go *inside* the closing quotation marks.

Be sure to indicate commas with a pause and periods with a longer pause. Use a different voice for the words of dialogue, and indicate the questions by your tone.

When I had eaten my corn I looked round. In the stall next to mine stood a little fat gray pony, with a thick mane and tail, a very pretty head, and a pert little nose. I put my head up to the iron rails at the top of my box, and said, "How do you do? What is your name?"

APPENDICES

APPENDIX 1
After Year Four

Once the student is able to do the final assignments in Year Four, she has mastered the basics of writing. She is ready to learn the techniques of putting her thoughts down on paper in a convincing, orderly fashion.

Her next step should be a middle-grade writing program which teaches skills in outlining, organizing, and diagramming. For recommendations, go to www.peacehillpress.com.

APPENDIX 2
Troubleshooting

Q. **My student cries when he writes. What do I do?**

A. A single day of crying just means you need to take a break, boost blood sugar, reassure the child, and regather. But if the student cries on a regular basis, it's a sign that the writing he's doing isn't developmentally appropriate.

Crying is an expression of nonverbal frustration. The student has no idea why he's crying; he just knows that something is wrong. His understanding of the writing process isn't sophisticated enough to locate the problem, so you need to help him out.

First: if you're using a particular writing program, sell it and try something else. Writing and mathematics are skill-based programs. The way in which the skill is presented *must* make sense to the child. If it isn't a match for the way the student thinks, it won't work (no matter how good it is).

Second: make sure that the student is able to narrate and take dictation. If he hasn't mastered one of these skills, he's probably crying because he can't figure out how to get words down on paper.

Third: if he's weeping over a journal or creative writing assignment, eliminate that part of your program. Every student needs to learn the skills of expository writing. But as a creative writer and writing teacher, I have become convinced that creative writing (which includes journaling) is something that some students are hardwired for—and others aren't. If the student isn't naturally inclined to creative writing, *don't force him to complete creative writing assignments.* You won't turn him into a creative writer, and you may turn him off the idea of writing *anything.*

Q. My student hates creative writing. How can I get him to do more of it?

A. See above. Creative writing *is not necessary.*

Q. My student hates his journal. What do I do?

A. Throw it away. (See above.)

Q. My student loves creative writing, but hates expository writing. What do I do?

A. Many creative writers behave like reluctant writers when they're faced with an expository assignment. The creative writing is a natural gift; the ability to think through information, organize it, and put it down on paper needs to be taught. Let your creative writer soar with stories and poems, but meanwhile, take her through the basic steps of narration and dictation to develop the foundation for her other writing skills.

Q. It takes forever for my son to physically write something down. He has to painstakingly form every letter, and he is easily distracted. Is this normal? How can I get him to progress with his writing when the smallest assignment takes him so long to complete?

A. Yes, this is normal. It's exasperating, but it's normal. Keep three things in mind.

1. Pursue a nibbled-to-death-by-ducks strategy. Make sure that he does some copywork *every single school day*—at a level that won't frustrate him. Even if it's only two words at a time, if he continually exercises those hand muscles, they will eventually become stronger. Meanwhile, do his narrations orally, and continue to write them down for him as long as you need to.

2. Remember that most writing programs seem to have been invented for girls. They require an amount of physical handwriting that is acutely painful for many boys, whose fine motor skills develop later. Be kind to your

little boys, and if a writing (or handwriting) program seems to be frustrating them, choose something else or reduce the amount of physical handwriting that's required.

3.   If he's still struggling when he begins fourth grade, teach him to type. Word processing will change his whole attitude towards writing.

Q. My seventh grader can't write at all, and I don't know where to start.

A. Try the following diagnostic tests.

First, ask the student to tell you what he wants to write. (Assure him that he won't have to write the words down; you want to find out whether he is able to complete the first part of the writing process, the task of putting ideas into words.) If he is unable to put his ideas into coherent, complete sentences, he has never learned how to assemble his ideas into a form which can even be put down on paper. This student should begin with the narration exercises in Year One, and should continue through them until he is able to answer the question "What was that passage about?" with three or four fluent, complete sentences (a goal reached by the end of Year Four).

Second, dictate two sentences to the student. Tell the student that you will read the two sentences three times, and that the student should then write the sentences down. If the student can do this without effort, there is no need to do either the copywork or dictation exercises in this book—although the student may still need practice in narration.

However, you may find that the student runs into one of two difficulties. He may put down a misspelled, wrongly punctuated version of the sentences. This demonstrates that the student has never learned how to picture written language properly in his head; he has no visual memory of correctly written sentences. This student will probably need to go all the way back to Year One and do some copywork before moving on to dictation, and should continue on through the dictation exercises of Year Four.

Second, you may find that the student is unable to remember the sentences long enough to put them down on paper. This is the kind of student who is often able to tell you fluently what he wants to write, but when you then say, "Great! Write that down!" asks, "What did I say?" He is unable to hold sentences in his head while he writes—and until he is able to do this, he will remain frustrated. This student need not go back to copywork, but should begin with the dictation exercises in Year Two and work all the way up through Year Four.

Finally, you may find that your student can tell you what he wants to write, and can take dictation, but struggles to get words down on paper anyway. For some reason, the student is unable to complete the process of writing.

This student probably doesn't need to do the exercises in Years One to Four at all. Instead, ask the student to tell a tape recorder what he wants to write, and then to play the tape back and take dictation from it. He may need to do this for some months, but eventually he'll realize that he doesn't need the tape recorder; he can simply tell himself what he wants to write, and then put the words down from his own mental "dictation."

Q. I've neglected to give any formal writing instruction up till now. My student writes stories for fun, but has never done any formal assignments. How can I catch up?

A. First, you need to discover the student's skill level. Follow the techniques in the answer above, and if one of the diagnostic tests reveals a difficulty, start the student on the appropriate level.

If the student doesn't have any difficulty with the diagnostic tests, she needs to begin with the middle-level skills outlined in the overview (pages 10–15). Even if she's in high school, it's necessary for her to master these skills before moving on to high-school-level exercises in rhetoric.

Suggestions for more advanced writing programs can be found at www.peacehillpress.com.

Q. My student can narrate and take dictation, but still can't put them together. What do I do?

A. Give the student a tape recorder. Have him tell the tape recorder what he wants to write. He can then play the narration back to himself and take it down as though it were dictation. Eventually, he'll be able to do away with the mechanical aid of the tape recorder.

APPENDIX 3
Frequently Asked Questions
About Writing, Curricula, and Related Issues

Q. Do I now have everything I need to teach my student to write?

A. Not quite. Language arts is a four-fold category, an odd grouping together of four areas of study: spelling, grammar, reading, and writing. Spelling and grammar are skill areas. Reading is a content area. Writing combines the two.

Writing skills have to be supported by other areas of the curriculum: most directly, phonics, reading, spelling, and English grammar.

Phonics. Young students should continue to work through a phonics program until the principles of sounding out words have been completely covered. This avoids the phenomenon of "fourth-grade slump." Often, a student will work through part of a phonics program and then begin reading, combining principles that have been learned with an intuitive grasp of how language works. If the phonics instruction then ceases, students may have trouble later; they can sail along until they begin to encounter literature that moves up a level of difficulty—typically around fourth grade—and then they may find themselves struggling. Forced to guess, they read more and more slowly and have more difficulty making sense of the words, and suddenly an eager reader becomes a reluctant reader. You can avoid the problem by finishing the phonics program. Then have the student read aloud to you often. If he has difficulty sounding out certain words, review the troublesome phonetic pattern until it becomes automatic.

Reading. Good writers are good readers. Once the student is reading, she should be given plenty of time to exercise this new skill.

To develop a good reader, parents should be familiar with the three levels of reading:

INSTRUCTIONAL LEVEL: Figuring out the skills of reading; difficult, but possible with support; requires direct teacher/parent help.

ON LEVEL: The student can operate independently with occasional help.

BELOW LEVEL: Easy, for-fun reading; free-time reading that increases speed.

Instructional reading is done during phonics instruction, while on-level reading is typically the reading done for literature, science, and history. You can give the student additional practice in on-level reading by using the Blackstone Audio ReadyReader program, which for a rental fee ships paper books plus recorded versions on tape or CD, read at a much slower speed than usual so that students can follow along.

Below-level reading is perhaps the most important for developing a good reader; parents should give students an hour or so a day to read whatever books they choose (even books that you may think are too easy). This teaches the student to enjoy reading as recreation and as habit. It increases speed and enjoyment.

Spelling. Spelling is phonics backwards. In phonics, the student learns: the letter combination *ea* says *ee*. In spelling, he learns: if you hear the sound *ee*, you can use the letter combination *ea* to spell it.

There are two approaches to spelling: dictate from your phonics program, or use a separate spelling program that teaches the rules of spelling.

You may not see a transference of rules to actual written work in the writing of elementary students. I wouldn't fret too much about that; don't ignore it either, but the ability to transfer information from one field to another develops over time. You can help this along by reminding the student of the rules. During writing exercises, allow the student to write in pencil, and if he misspells, remind him of the rule, ask him to repeat it after you, and then allow him to erase and correct.

Grammar. Grammar is a foundational language skill which should be studied early, so that it can become part of the student's mental framework.

When students are in grades one through four, their minds are in a very receptive state, particularly in regards to language. You probably know that if you teach a student a foreign language in grades one through four, he is much more likely to be fluent and speak without accent than if you teach it later on. That's because the pathways in the brain that govern language learning are still developing. Since written language is a set of artificial conventions that govern the way we put words on paper, learning it is like learning a foreign language. So treat writing as you would a foreign language, and think to yourself: the sooner this student masters the code that governs written language, the sooner it will become second nature to him.

The goal is that the student will never have to stop to think about what form of a verb to use, which punctuation to put around a speech, whether or not to indent. Every time the student stops to think about the form of the language, rather than the ideas, he is halting the flow of his thought and is more likely to struggle. You want to make grammar part of the mental structure that the student uses when he writes—so that middle-grade writing, when he really begins to work hard at *ordering* ideas, will not also become a time when he is struggling to remember the basic rules of written language.

Grammar learning should be mostly oral in grades one and two. Use a grammar program (see the list of resources beginning on p. 241) oriented towards oral learning; in third and fourth grades, the student can begin to do workbook exercises, but if fine motor skills are still an issue, you should feel free to continue to do the exercises orally.

By grade five at the latest, the student should be in a full-fledged, skills-oriented grammar program that provides training in outlining and in diagramming (also listed beginning on p. 245). A word of caution: don't do the writing exercises, since most good grammar programs don't have an equally well-thought-out writing sequence. Anyway, doing those writing exercises as well as your writing program will wear the student out.

For a more detailed discussion of developing the other elementary-level language skills and programs, see *The Well-Trained Mind.*

Q. Once I finish this book, what do I do then?

A.   For a list of middle-grade and high-school programs that meet some of the criteria laid out here, go to www.peacehillpress.com.

Q. What about word processing?

A.   Students should probably continue to handwrite their assignments through Year Three or Four, since the physical act of writing reinforces the skills they're learning. By about fifth grade, though, I'd quit fighting that battle and teach them to type. However, DISABLE any spell-check or grammar-check tools in your word processing program. These encourage students to be lazy and sloppy in the knowledge that the tool will catch their mistakes. Unfortunately, spelling- and grammar-check programs are wrong far too frequently to be of real value.

The student should also continue to pursue a penmanship program, since legible handwriting is a valuable adult skill. However, allowing him to type his writing assignments can remove a roadblock in the path towards mature writing.

Q. My student is learning cursive. Should I require her to do her writing assignments in cursive now?

A.   Ideally, but you don't want this to hinder her. You could begin by asking her to do part of her writing assignments in cursive, and gradually phase in cursive for all writing. But be sure not to put unnecessary roadblocks in the way of the writing process. It would be better for her to continue to print, than to be frustrated by the task of putting her narrations into cursive.

Q. Should I worry about the style of my student's writing?

A. Not in my opinion. Good style is an outgrowth of clear thinking, and plain style is the best style of all. The emphasis on copywork and dictation in *Writing with Ease: Strong Fundamentals* gives the student plenty of excellent style models; as long as the student is practicing putting these words down on paper, you can afford to wait and allow her to develop her own individual style.

Q. **What about those three stages of writing—first fundamentals, then organization and analysis, and finally rhetoric? What are they based on?**

A. The three stages of writing are based on the traditional pattern of classical education. During the first stage of education, children are very retentive and enjoy memorization, but most children do not have a well-developed critical ability; this is the time to lay the building blocks of learning, the foundation for later accomplishment. In the second stage, or middle grade, then students begin to develop a critical and analytical ability; this is the time for them to begin to think critically about the ordering of their own ideas. The final stage of education, the high-school years, are a time when students are encouraged to express opinions and draw conclusions. For a much more detailed explanation, visit www.welltrainedmind.com or see *The Well-Trained Mind: A Guide to Classical Education at Home,* by Jessie Wise and Susan Wise Bauer.

Although this method of teaching writing is attractive to parents and teachers who are already committed to using the classical pattern, it can also be used by any parent or teacher. A full-fledged commitment to classical education is not necessary.

Q. **Should I correct the writing my student does for fun?**

A. Absolutely not. Praise it and ignore all mistakes.

Q. **What about word study?**

A. The study of word derivations might be useful, but I'm not sure that vocabulary-building workbooks are of much use. We use and remember the words we learn in context. Reading is a much more valuable vocabulary-builder. As Erasmus wrote in his classical text *Copia,* "You will learn to exercise judgment [in word choice] by carefully observing elegant and appropriate diction, while the assiduous reading of every type of author will allow you to fill your store....So the first thing is to extract the best words one can from every type of writer, and whatever they like, add them to the collection..." In other words, when you find words in your reading, you know their shade of meaning, their slight distinction in emphasis, their level of formality or informality: these are things it is almost impossible to get through a word study program.

Q. What is the progymnasmata?

A.   It is a series of exercises meant to prepare classical rhetoricians for full-scale arguments. As such, it belongs primarily in the third phase of writing—the high-school, or rhetoric, stage. See page 16.

Q. Why are the progymnasmata you use different from exercises in other classical rhetoric courses?

A.   The progymnasmata were not a standardized "curriculum." Every ancient teacher of rhetoric differed in his use of the exercises, and medieval and Renaissance rhetoricians altered ancient traditions to make the exercises more useful for medieval and Renaissance students. I have chosen those progymnasmata exercises which contribute the most to the student's development as a beginning writer of persuasive, expository essays. More progymnasmata exercises—many of which are no longer particularly useful to modern writers—can be found in ancient rhetoric texts, as well as in college-level rhetoric texts such as *Classical Rhetoric for the Modern Student* by Edward Corbett and Robert Connors (4th edition, Oxford University Press, 1998) and *The New Oxford Guide to Writing* by Thomas Kane (Oxford University Press, 1994).

APPENDIX 4
Resources

For alternative recommendations and more resources and information, see *The Well-Trained Mind: A Guide to Classical Education at Home*, by Jessie Wise and Susan Wise Bauer (rev. ed., W. W. Norton, 2004).

Preschool and Kindergarten Resources

Beginning Handwriting Programs

Zaner-Bloser *Handwriting* series. Order from www.zaner-bloser.com. This handwriting series uses a continuous-stroke alphabet that doesn't require a huge shift from print to cursive.

Handwriting without Tears. Order from www.hwtears.com. Designed by Jan Olsen, this is useful for students who find handwriting particularly difficult.

Phonics Programs

The Ordinary Parent's Guide to Teaching Reading, by Jessie Wise and Sara Buffington (Peace Hill Press, 2004). This phonics program doesn't require any handwriting and is scripted, so that the parent/teacher has plenty of guidance in presenting the required skills. Order from www.peacehillpress.com.

Phonics Pathways, by Dolores Hiskes (9th ed., Jossey-Bass, 2005). Order from any bookstore. This phonics program is unscripted, for parents/teachers who prefer to handle the explanations themselves.

Audiobooks

Toddler and older

Hoban, Russell. *The Frances Audio Collection*, read by Glynis Johns.

Lobel, Arnold. *Frog and Toad Audio Collection*, read by Arnold Lobel (Audible.com).

_____. *Grasshopper on the Road*, read by Arnold Lobel.

_____.   *Mouse Soup*, read by Arnold Lobel.

McCloskey, Robert. *Blueberries for Sal*, read by Frank Scardino.

Minarik, Else Holmelund. *Little Bear Audio Collection*, read by Sigourney Weaver.

Zion, Gene. *Harry and the Lady Next Door*, read by Becca Lish.

K4 and older

Andersen, Hans Christian. *The Ugly Duckling and Other Stories*, read by Rebecca Burns (Audible.com).

_____. *Andersen's Fairy Tales*, read by Erica Johns (Audible.com).

Favorite Children's Stories, various readers (Blackstone Audio).

Gruelle, Johnny. *Raggedy Ann and Raggedy Andy Stories*, read by Swoosie Kurtz and Cicely Tyson (Audible.com).

Kingston, Rosemary. *Fifty Famous Fairy Tales*, read by Marguerite Gavin (Blackstone Audio, Audible.com).

MacDonald, Betty. *Mrs. Piggle-Wiggle*, read by John McDonough.

Milne, A. A. *Winnie-the-Pooh, The House at Pooh Corner, When We Were Very Young & Now We Are Six*, read by Peter Dennis (Blackstone Audio, Audible.com).

Potter, Beatrix. *Tales of Beatrix Potter*, read by Nadia May (Blackstone Audio, Audible.com).

_____. *The Complete Tales of Beatrix Potter*, read by Shelly Frasier (Audible.com).

K5 and older

Baum, L. Frank. *The Wizard of Oz*, read by Anna Fields (Blackstone Audio).

_____. *The Patchwork Girl of Oz*, various readers (Blackstone Audio).

_____. *The Land of Oz*, read by Anna Fields (Blackstone Audio).

Bond, Michael. *A Bear Called Paddington*, read by Stephen Fry (Audible.com).

Carroll, Lewis. *Alice in Wonderland*, read by Christopher Plummer.

_____. *Alice Through the Looking-Glass*, read by Christopher Plummer.

Cleary, Beverly. *The Mouse and the Motorcycle*, read by William Roberts.

Collodi, Carlo. *Pinocchio*, read by Susan O'Malley (Blackstone Audio).

Grahame, Kenneth. *The Wind in the Willows*, read by Mary Woods (Blackstone Audio).

Kipling, Rudyard. *Just So Stories*, read by Johanna Ward (Blackstone Audio).

Lewis, C. S. *Chronicles of Narnia*, unabridged (HarperAudio, Audible.com).

Nesbit, Edith. *Five Children and It*, read by Johanna Ward (Blackstone Audio).

Sewell, Anna. *Black Beauty*, read by John Chatty (Blackstone Audio).

Sidney, Margaret. *The Five Little Peppers and How They Grew*, read by Grace Conlin (Blackstone Audio).

Smith, Dodie. *The 101 Dalmations*, read by Martin Jarvis (Audible.com).

Spyri, Johanna. *Heidi*, read by Johanna Ward (Blackstone Audio).

Travers, Pamela L. *Mary Poppins*, read by Sophie Thompson.

White, E. B. *Charlotte's Web*, read by E. B. White (Audible.com).

Resources for Elementary Students

Phonics

The Ordinary Parent's Guide to Teaching Reading, by Jessie Wise and Sara Buffington (Peace Hill Press, 2004). This phonics program doesn't require any handwriting and is scripted, so that the parent/teacher has plenty of guidance in presenting the required skills. Order from www.peacehillpress.com.

Phonics Pathways, by Dolores Hiskes (9th ed., Jossey-Bass, 2005). Order from any bookstore. This phonics program is unscripted, for parents/teachers who prefer to handle the explanations themselves.

Audiobooks

Blackstone Audio's ReadyReader program is found at www.blackstoneaudio.com/readyreader.cfm.

Other good audiobook selections for young listeners (all are available through Blackstone Audio and Audible.com):

Alexander, Lloyd. *The Prydain Chronicles.*

Barrie, J. M. *Peter Pan.*

Burnett, Frances Hodgson. *The Secret Garden.*

_____. *A Little Princess.*

Colum, Padraic. *The Children's Homer.*

_____. *The Golden Fleece and the Heroes Who Lived Before Achilles.*

Dahl, Roald. *Fantastic Mr. Fox.*

Dickens, Charles. *A Christmas Carol.*

Eager, Edward. *Half Magic.*

Estes, Eleanor. *The Moffats.*

Forbes, Esther. *Johnny Tremain.*

Green, Roger Lancelyn. *The Tale of Troy.*

Jacques, Brian. *The Redwall Chronicles.*

Kipling, Rudyard. *The Jungle Book.*

Konigsburg, E. J. *From the Mixed-up Files of Mrs. Basil E. Frankweiler.*

Lindgren, Astrid. *Pippi Longstocking.*

Lofting, Hugh. *The Story of Doctor Dolittle.*

_____. *The Voyages of Doctor Dolittle.*

Montgomery, L. M. *Anne of Green Gables.*

_____. *Anne of Avonlea .*

_____. *The Story Girl.*

_____. *Emily of New Moon .*

Nesbit, Edith. *The Railway Children.*

_____. *The Story of the Treasure Seekers.*

_____. *The Enchanted Castle.*

North, Sterling. *Rascal.*

Norton, Mary. *The Borrowers.*

Speare, Elizabeth George. *The Bronze Bow.*

Stevenson, Robert Louis. *Kidnapped.*

_____. *Treasure Island.*

Streatfeild, Noel. *Ballet Shoes.*

White, E. B. *Stuart Little.*

Wyss, Johann David. *The Swiss Family Robinson.*

Spelling Resources

Modern Curriculum Press *Spelling Workout* series (rev. ed., Pearson Learning Group, 2001). Order from www.pearsonlearning.com.

Spelling Power, by Beverly L. Adams-Gordon (3rd ed., Castlemoyle Press,

1997). Order from www.castlemoyle.com.

Grammar Resources

First Language Lessons for the Well-Trained Mind, Level One, by Jessie Wise (Peace Hill Press, 2010). Order from www.peacehillpress.com. *First Language Lessons* is a complete beginning grammar text that uses copywork, narration, picture study, and other classical techniques to develop the young student's language ability. Scripted lessons give the teacher direction and confidence, while exquisite pencil reproductions of great paintings are used to encourage children in oral composition. This oral language text covers first-grade grammar.

First Language Lessons for the Well-Trained Mind, Level Two, by Jessie Wise (Peace Hill Press, 2010). Order from www.peacehillpress.com. This oral language text covers second-grade grammar.

First Language Lessons for the Well-Trained Mind, Level Three, by Jessie Wise and Sara Buffington (Peace Hill Press, 2007). Order from www.peacehillpress.com. This language text covers third-grade grammar.

First Language Lessons for the Well-Trained Mind, Level Four, by Jessie Wise and Sara Buffington (Peace Hill Press, 2008). Order from www.peacehillpress.com. This language text covers fourth-grade grammar.

Rod & Staff *Grammar and Composition* (Rod and Staff, 1991 and following). Order from www.rainbowresource.com. This grammar program can be followed from third grade on.

Bibliography of Excerpts

Adams, Capt. F. Colburn. *The Siege of Washington, D.C.: Written Expressly for Little People.* New York: Dick & Fitzgerald, 1867. Available from Kessinger Publishing (Whitefish, MT), 2004. Year Four, Week 11.

Aesop. *The Aesop for Children.* Chicago: Rand McNally & Co., 1919. Available from Scholastic (New York), 1994. Year Two, Week 1.

Alcott, Louisa May. *Little Women.* Boston: A. K. Loring, 1868. Available from Signet Press (New York) as a Signet Classic Edition, 2004. Year Four, Week 11.

Andersen, Hans Christian. *Andersen's Fairy Tales.* New York: Holt, Rinehart & Winston, 1926. Available as *Hans Andersen's Fairy Tales: A Selection* from Oxford University Press (Oxford), 1998. Year Four, Week 1.

Baldwin, James. *Fifty Famous People.* New York: American Book Company, 1912. Available from Yesterday's Classics (Chapel Hill, NC), 2005. Year Four, Week 20.

Barrie, J. M. *Peter and Wendy.* New York: Charles Scribner's Sons, 1911. Available as *Peter Pan* from Viking Press (New York), 1991. Year Two, Week 36.

Baum, L. Frank. *The Magic of Oz.* Chicago: Reilly & Lee, 1919. Available from Dover Publications (New York), 1998. Year Two, Week 28.

————. *The Wonderful Wizard of Oz.* Chicago: George M. Hill, 1900. Available from Harper Collins (New York), 2000. Year One, Week 36.

Carroll, Lewis. *Alice's Adventures in Wonderland.* New York: Macmillan, 1865. Available from Signet Press (New York) in a Signet Classic Edition as *Alice's Adventures in Wonderland and Through the Looking-Glass* (2000). Year One, Week 4.
————. *Alice Through the Looking Glass.* New York: Macmillan, 1872. See above. Year Three, Week 20.

Defoe, Daniel. *The Life and Adventures of Robinson Crusoe.* London: W. Taylor, 1719. Available as *Robinson Crusoe* from Penguin (New York), 2003. Year Four, Week 28.

Franklin, Benjamin. *The Autobiography of Benjamin Franklin.* London: J. Parsons, 1793. Available from Dover (New York), 1996. Year Four, Week 20.

Green, Roger Lancelyn. *Tales of Ancient Egypt.* New York: Puffin Books, 1970. Year Three, Week 11.

Grimm, Jacob, and Wilhelm Grimm. *Tales from the Brothers Grimm*, trans. Edgar Taylor and Marian Edwardes. London: Dent & Dutton, 1936. Available as *The Complete Grimm's Fairy Tales* from Pantheon Books (New York), 1976. Year Three, Week 1.

Herodotus. *The Histories,* trans. Robin Waterfield. Oxford: Oxford University Press, 1998. Year Three, Week 11.

Hillyer, V.M. *A Child's Geography of the World.* New York, NY: the Century Company, 1929. Revised by Edward G. Huey and republished by Appleton-Century-Crofts, 1951. Year One, Week 20.

Johnston, Harry. *Pioneers in Canada.* London: Blackie and Son, 1912. Available from BiblioBazaar (Charleston, SC), 2007. Year Three, Week 28.

Lawson, Robert. *Rabbit Hill.* New York: Dell Publishing Co., 1944. Available from Puffin (New York), 2007. Year Three, Week 36.

McGuffey, William H., ed. *Fourth Eclectic Reader.* New York: American Book Company, 1920. Available as *McGuffey's Fourth Eclectic Reader* from Hard Press (Lenox, MA), 2006. Year Four, Week 20.

Milne, A. A. *The House at Pooh Corner.* New York: E. P. Dutton & Co., 1928. Available as *The World of Pooh: The Complete Winnie-the-Pooh and The House at Pooh Corner* from Dutton (New York), 1988. Year One, Week 20.

————. *Winnie-the-Pooh.* New York: E. P. Dutton & Co., 1926. See above. Year One, Week 20.

Montgomery, Lucy Maud. *Anne of Green Gables.* Boston: L. C. Page & Co., 1908. Available in a Signet Classic Edition from Signet (New York), 2003. Year Three, Week 28.

Nesbit, Edith. *Five Children and It.* London: Dodd, Mead & Co., 1905. Available as A Yearling Classic from Dell Publishing Co., 1986. Year Two, Week 19.

Sewell, Anna. *Black Beauty: The Autobiography of a Horse.* London: Jarrold & Sons, 1877. Available from Scholastic (New York), 2003. Year Four, Week 36.

Smith, Dodie. *The 101 Dalmatians.* London: Heinemann, 1956. Available from Barnes & Noble (New York), 1996. Year Two, Week 11.

Stevenson, Robert Louis. *A Child's Garden of Verses.* London: Longmans, Green & Co., 1885. Available as a Penguin Popular Classic from Penguin (New York), 1995. Year One, Week 36.

White, E. B. *The Trumpet of the Swan.* New York: Harper Trophy, 1970. Year One, Week 11.

Wilder, Laura Ingalls. *Little House in the Big* Woods. New York: Harper &

Brothers, 1932. Available from HarperTrophy (New York), 2007. Year One, Week 1.

————. *Little House on the Prairie.* New York: Harper & Brothers, 1935. Available from HarperTrophy (New York), 2007. Year One, Week 28.

————. *On the Banks of Plum Creek.* New York: Harper & Brothers, 1937. Available from HarperTrophy (New York), 2007. Year One, Week 28.

Index